in his own words

Keith Richards

Mick St. Michael

OMNIBUS PRESS
LONDON · NEW YORK · PARIS · SYDNEY · COPENHAGEN · MADRID

Edited by Chris Charlesworth.
Cover & book designed by Michael Bell Design.
Picture research by David Brolan.

ISBN 0.7119.3634.X
Order No. OP 47492

Exclusive Distributors:
Book Sales Limited
8/9 Frith Street,
London W1V 5TZ, UK.

Music Sales Corporation
257 Park Avenue South,
New York, NY 10010, USA.

Music Sales Pty Limited
120 Rothschild Avenue,
Rosebery, NSW 2018, Australia.

To the Music Trade only:
Music Sales Limited
8/9 Frith Street,
London W1V 5TZ, UK.

Photo credits: Richie Aaron/Redferns: 45b, 61t; John Bellimisso/Retna: 56; Dominick Conde/
Star File: 71, 73t, 76; Fin Costello/Redferns: 17, 50b, 70t, 96; George Gobes/Star File: 43t;
Harry Goodwin: 14b, 22, 31, 53, 68, 90b; Bob Gruen/Star File: 4, 60, 70b, 73b, 74, 86, 91, 93;
London Features International: front cover, back cover t, 7, 11, 13, 19, 20, 24, 30, 34, 45t, 46c&b,
47t&b, 48t, 49b, 50t&c, 51t&b, 52, 61b, 64, 65, 69, 75t&b, 77, 79, 90t, 95t&b; Music Sales Archives:
8, 16b, 21t, 23, 38b, 39t, 44, 66b, 67, 89; Pictorial Press: 6, 10, 14t, 15, 16t, 26, 37, 46; Barry Plummer:
32, 43b, 57, 92; Neal Preston/Retna: 42b; Chuck Pulin/Star File: 28, 33, 72, 84b; Michael Putland/
Retna: 39b, 78, 80; David Redfern/Redferns: 42t, 62; Redferns: 27,63; Retna: 36, 40, 87, 54;
Ebet Roberts/Redferns: back cover b, 18, 25, 29, 38t, 49t, 55, 58, 59, 82, 83, 85; David Seelig/Star File:
88; Joe Sia/Star File: 12, 41; Star File: 94; Luciano Viti/Retna: 81; G. Wiltshire/Redferns: 21b;
Vinnie Zuffante/Star File: 35, 48b, 66t, 84t

Printed by Scotprint Limited, Musselburgh, Edinburgh.

A catalogue record for this book is available from the British Library.

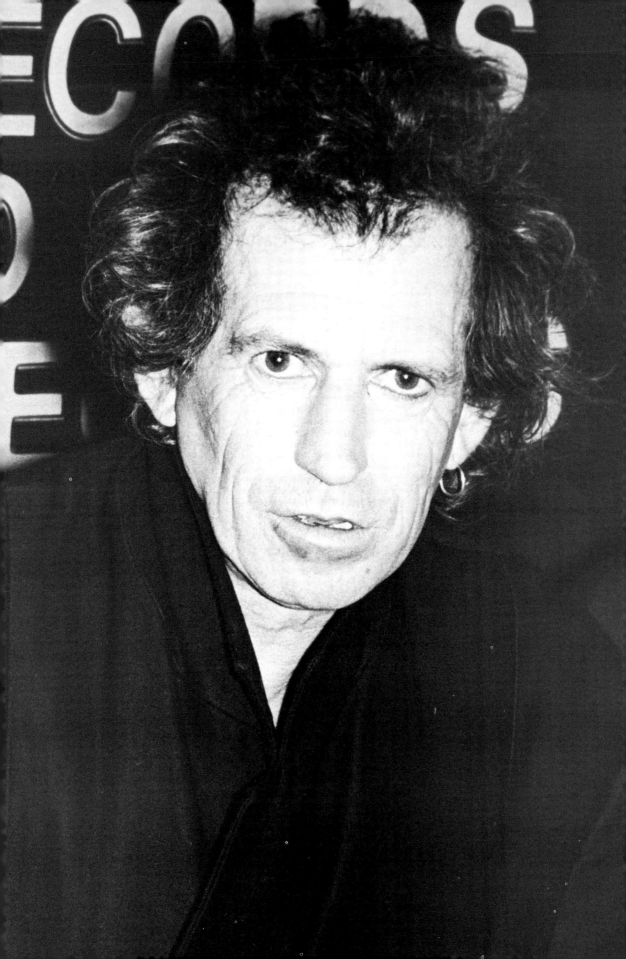

Introduction

**"I don't think I'm anything special.
Just a regular rock'n'roll myth? Yeah." (1992)**

Few musicians embody the spirit of rock'n'roll so completely
as Keith Richards. Aside from his great musical contribution, his
unkempt, debauched, wasted appearance is the supreme ideal to which
to aspire for scores of leather clad rockers who have tried to follow
in Keith's illustrious footsteps.

He was there from the very beginning, as the Stones sought to make
their first footholds in the closed, incestuous London R&B scene... he
was there when they scandalised authority by peeing on filling-station
forecourts... he was there when they dressed in drag to promote
'Have You Seen Your Mother'. And he was very much there when
the authorities tried to 'break a butterfly on a wheel', as the famous
Times editorial put it, and jailed the Glimmer Twins, Jagger and
Richards, for alleged drugs offences.

Many thought drugs would be his downfall. A self-confessed heroin
user, he went through the card of available pharmaceuticals yet remained
resolutely wedded to this mortal coil. Brian Jones and Mick Taylor
departed, the former all too permanently, yet the Stones' guitar
department remained very much open for business. It was Keith who
filled the gap by bringing close friend Ronnie Wood into the fold,
a musical marriage so successful that the ex-Face has now clocked up
more years as a Stone than his predecessors combined. Punk came
and went, but Keith was still there, again inspiring the likes of
Johnny Thunders and countless others with his inimitable sartorial
and musical style.

In the Eighties, rumours of blood transfusions and rifts with Jagger
abounded. More certain was marriage to model Patti Hansen after the
split with long-time girlfriend Anita Pallenberg. As the Stones seemed
forever on the point of disintegration, Keith finally broke a long-time
vow and did his own thing, while stressing that his commitment to the
Stones as a going concern remained unwavering. And as Bill Wyman
threatened to jump ship and become only the third ex-Stone, it was
clear that as long as Jagger and Richards remained the band would roll
along regardless.

Now in the Nineties, with the Stones freshly signed to Virgin Records,
Keith the human riff continues to power them to future glory. And the
preponderance of Keef wannabes, from The Black Crowes to The Spin
Doctors and beyond, underlines the fact that his love affair with the
guitar - not his drug intake - will be Richards' lasting legacy.

Mick Jagger may be the most quoted Stone but Mick is a politician
and what he has to say is frequently inconsequential or stunted by his
unwillingness to become involved in controversy. Keith has never
been a politician and when he speaks he keeps little back. If all you
know of him is the much-imitated 'Keef riff', prepare for a surprise...

The Band

Early Days

"You wouldn't have liked to have fucking lived there (with Mick Jagger and Brian Jones in Edith Grove in Chelsea). It was *disgusting*. Mould growing on the walls and no-one was ever going to clean the joint up. We lived on the second floor and on the ground floor there were these four students - chick teachers from Sheffield and Nottingham who got roped into doing the cleaning and occasionally got knocked off for their trouble. They had no sympathy for what was going on on our floor. But, oh man, it was filthy! I had the tape recorder rigged up on the toilet. I had these amazing tapes of people on the john which I'd play the next day. It's incredible what people do while they're taking a crap. It was the funniest… you'd get people muttering, 'Whoah, I need that. Ooooah! Just made it! Mmmm! Larvely!' Ah, youthful high jinx." (1988)

"At the time we started none of us were concerned with making it, we were dedicated to furthering and making known this music we absolutely loved. All we wanted to do was play. With luck, break even and have some regular gigs. That's as far as our ambition went. Success never came into it. We never dreamed of it, never even thought we could turn the whole of London to do what we were doing, let alone the rest of the world. We didn't even think like that. We thought finding somewhere to play would be nice one night a week where a few people could dance. Suddenly one night became a week which became a month. The whole thing just exploded."

"We hadn't got any gigs. Nothing to do. We'd spend hours at a time just making faces at each other, Brian was always the best at that. There was a particularly horrible one he could do by pulling his eyes down at the corners and sticking his fingers up his nostrils. He called it 'doing a Nanker'."

"We just starved and listened to the blues and played all day and slept all night and tried to get gigs. At the time we thought the absolute pinnacle of success would be maybe three or four regular club gigs in London. We kind of knew that this wouldn't play in Leicester or even Watford! Who's going to listen to this imitation Muddy Waters and Jimmy Reed outside of London? We figured that the impossible dream was four gigs a week in the centre of London.

"We knew that no-one else was doing it and we were the best
and most together band at it. The problem was getting the gigs in the
back rooms of pubs and knocking the traditional jazz guys off their
slots because they jealously guarded their gigs. A lot of little vicious
moves went down behind the scene. A bunch of upstarts trying to take
your living from you. At the time when you're 18 you don't think of
it like that. And there were these old guys, maybe 25, trying to hang
on to their gigs." (1988)

"Alexis (Korner) would hustle me off the stage after a couple of
numbers. He was anxious to get hold of Mick for himself so in various
subtle ways he wouldn't let me stay on there long. Obviously Alexis
didn't want another guitarist but he did want a flash, young singer.
Also you got a lot more money on the debutante circuit which Korner
often played. Consequently there was a period when Brian and I felt
that Mick was gonna go off and leave us. It was a drag to think about
because we really knew that we had something going. But we also
figured that Mick knew that too."

"Between Mick, Brian and myself, we were pretty determined.
There was no other way for it to go except up. Since we were
determined that we were going to stick together and play, and since
we were down to thieving potatoes out of supermarkets anyway, and
selling beer bottles back to the off-licence, there was nothing else to
do except push on. It had to get better, even if it didn't get fantastic.

It was difficult, but it was fun too. We were only 19 or something. We didn't give a shit anyway." (1973)

Rolling On

"We've been very very lucky in that we've got a band that can live together and work together and sometimes not see each other for months on end and still make it groove. I don't know if I could take it if I had to live all the bullshit that seems to go down when bands break up… There aren't many drummers like Charlie Watts who can play rock'n'roll and other things and still swing which is the basic thing. That goes for the rhythm section as a whole… I sometimes sway between being a prisoner and an outcast. I'm not sure whether they're keeping me in or pushing me out. You have to put so much effort and organisation into breaking any of those well-trodden paths… I'm not a junkie." (1977)

"Well if anyone can come back after such a long lay off, the Stones can. It's still the question I get asked most all the time, everywhere – when are you getting back together? When is it going to happen? People certainly want us to. In a way the longer the gap, the greater the fascination. It's a unique situation. The weird thing is with the Stones – at least until we stopped working – there was still an incredible spectrum of fans. There'd be grandmas with their daughters and granddaughters in the audience. Whooah, lovely! Three generations!
    "Depending on who you talk to, some people think The Rolling Stones started with 'Brown Sugar', some think there wasn't a Rolling Stones before 'Start Me Up'. Others think 'Satisfaction' was the first record. It's weird when you are part of something that's gone on that long and you realise that you've got something that people have grown up with. A lot of people haven't known a world without The Rolling Stones. They're as much a part of life as your mum or your dad or the television set or the armchair or the air you breathe. You're born into the world and there are The Rolling Stones. That's very hard to take in." (1988)

"I've got their weird double feelings about all the Stones' myths and adventures, because I understand how they're perceived by the outside world and yet, obviously, I was right at the centre of things. It's staggering when I reflect on the guys I've known and the things that have happened. But it's part of my life, so I don't go into deep thoughts about it every day. But sometimes, you double-take and it's like, 'Wow!' And then, other times, I'll see my name in bookshops and I'll think, 'What am I doing there?' It's weird talking to younger guys. The Stones have been there throughout their whole lives, in everybody's room. For me, it's like knowing everybody - in a way." (1992)

The Boys In The Band

MICK

First meeting

"I knew Mick when we were really young…five, six, seven.
Then I moved and didn't see him for a long time.

"And one day I met Jagger again, of all places on the fucking train.
I was going to school and he was going to the London School of
Economics; it was about 1960. Under his arm he had four or five
albums. We recognised each other straight off. 'Hi man', I say. 'Where
ya going?' he says. And under his arm he's got Chuck Berry and Little
Walter, Muddy Waters. 'You're into Chuck Berry, man?' That's a
coincidence. He said, 'Yeah, I got a few more albums, been writing
away to this, uh, Chess Records in Chicago and got a mailing list…'

"So I invited him to my place for a cup of tea. He started playing
me these records and I really turned onto it. We were both still living
in Dartford, on the edge of London."

Competition and rivalry

"Competition has always been unnecessary between us. It's never
been there before. And it's unnecessary except Mick seems eager to
create that atmosphere. It's not even only me. Mick will knock
something or say the opposite just because he wants to put his mark
on everything.

"I don't think we have that much of a competition. You've
got to be co-operative and sometimes you've got to be competitive.
Perhaps it's very much a part of being brought up the wrong way.
I'm not particularly keen on competitions. It's a negative incentive
because if you win then the other person loses. You can always
win by tricking everybody all the time. I don't care 'cause I know
I can win by trickery. And what's the point? I don't find it
particularly clever."

"Mick's and my battles are not exactly as perceived through the
press or other people. They're far more convoluted, because we've
known each other for most of our lives - I mean, since we were four
or five. So they involve a lot more subtleties and ins and outs than can
possibly be explained. But I think there is on Mick's part a bit of a
Peter Pan complex. It's a hard job, being the front man. In order to
do it, you've got to think in a way that you're semi-divine…

"Last month or so, I've been in touch with the other Stones.
Mick suddenly called up, and the rest of them: 'Let's put the Stones
back together.' I'm thinking, I'm in the middle of an album.
Now what are you trying to do? Screw me up?" (1988)

"I don't understand where this thing came from that makes it necessary to compete with me. Or even why it happened. Anything I do he's gotta negate. He's been very dictatorial to everybody lately whereas before the studio was run on a much more co-operative basis. Now it's automatic negativity that is the basic thing I get from Mick."

"When I cleaned up and 'Emotional Rescue' time came around - 'Hey I'm back, I'm clean, I'm ready; I'm back to help and take some of that weight off your shoulders' - immediately I got a sense of resentment. Whereas I felt that he would be happy to unburden himself of some of that shit, he felt that I was homing in and trying to take control. And that's when I first sensed the feeling of discontent, shall we say.

   "It wasn't intended like that from my point of view, but that's when I first got a feeling that he's got so used to running the show that there was no way he was going to give it up." (1988)

"The only things Mick and I disagree about is the band, the music and what we do."

"Whatever pressure I'm going through can't be anything like the pressure Mick's going through to be so unsure of what he's doing by automatically putting me down. Mick is a selfish person but he's not ungenerous. In many ways he's a really nice guy. But he's too unsure of himself to be that nice guy."

Mick the man

"I love Mick. Most of my efforts with Mick go to trying to open his eyes: 'You don't need to do this. You have no problem, all you need to do is just grow up with it'." (1988)

"Mick communicates to the audience from a very safe distance. The distance between him and 20,000 people is just a matter of exaggerating a façade without actually letting anybody know anything about you. Mick has got to be more real with people."

"Mick should stop trying to be Peter Pan. I don't see the point of trying to be 25 when you are not - he's obsessed with his age." (1987)

"Mick always says he wants an office with a secretary. He doesn't feel he has to always go to the office but he loves the fuckin' place. That's a real English bourgeois hang-up - to have a secretary and all that 'I'm at the office darling'."

"Instead of getting more secure over the years, which you think Mick would have every right to, he's getting more insecure.

Bianca Jagger

Unfortunately he's taking it out on the wrong people. Of course the person who's got a problem is the last one to realise it. I guess like everything else, it will work itself out."

"I always had lots of energy. Mick thinks he's hyper and that he's got a lot of energy but he hasn't. He's got a quick flash in him but no stamina. Have you ever seen Mick after he's stayed up for one night? Forget it."

"If you're Mick Jagger you should be able to enjoy your life a little better. You should be a little less hung-up about being Mick Jagger, although I understand fully that being the front man of the Stones or any big band is an incredibly hard task." (1988)

"I don't think anything about them (Jagger's solo albums). Personally, I don't think he should think anything about them either." (1988)

"Since she married Mick, Bianca is enormous. Everyone knows Bianca. She's in Vogue, the newspapers, but it's not something you do, it's not a job, it's not an art to get yourself in the papers. What have you created? Somebody that's always good for an airport picture on page three."

"I think (Bianca)'s had a bigger negative influence on Mick than anyone would have thought possible. Mick, Anita and I used to go around an awful lot before he met Bianca."
"Because everybody has a different idea of what or who Mick Jagger is, he's confused himself now as to who he actually is. People are usually too embarrassed or don't want to get involved that much to let Mick know. I'm one of them. It is a tremendous hassle to keep Mick in reality because he is so easily influenced."

"Mick's got to stop slapping paint all over his face to that absurd Japanese theatre degree. Mick is getting older and he's got to find a way to mature if he's gonna do what he does. He's got to stop running around the stage and getting himself out of breath in the first ten minutes. He's got to get in front of that fuckin' mike and sing.
   "Goddamn it, if you're gonna do a two-hour show you can start off real easy. You've got all the time in the world. You don't have to give it all away at once. I pace the music but I can't pace Jagger."

Bigger than both of us

"I tip my hat to Mick a lot. I admire the guy enormously. In the Seventies, when I was on dope and I would do nothing but put the songs together and turn up and not deal with any other business of the

Stones, Mick took all of that work on his shoulders and did it all and covered my ass. And I've always admired him for that. I mean, he did exactly what a friend should do." (1988)

"Why have Mick and I stayed together all this time? Well, we do so somewhat reluctantly.

"It's when we stop working that Mick and I start sniping and bickering at each other. There are hundreds of things that Mick and I vehemently disagree upon, but the minute we start working again… If we sit down in a room together with just a keyboard and guitar, all that stuff suddenly becomes totally irrelevant.

"You see, Mick and I recognise the fact that for some unknown reason, without putting too much effort into it, within an hour we'll have two or three good ideas worked out for future songs.

"I know it's a cliché, but every time Mick and I get back together to tour, to record or whatever, it really is a question of this thing is bigger than the both of us!" (1991)

"In Paris I live around the corner from the English bookshop and there was this book in there and in great gold letters it said Brenda Jagger. So he became Brenda for a bit. That was at the time of 'Dirty Work' when he was spending more time doing his solo stuff instead of doing 'Dirty Work', which really pissed me off. He shouldn't have been making the album if he wasn't into it. I very nearly stiffed him at the time. But there's no joy in punching a wimp. I like him, and I say these things, and they come out and they sound kind of cruel but I've known Mick since I was four years old. And despite myself, I do love the guy." (1988)

"Mick and I always prided ourselves on recognising the point when you thought you had become bigger than The Rolling Stones." (1988)

BRIAN

His life

"Brian's only solution became clinging to either Mick or me, which created a triangle of sorts. It was like Brian's open wound. Eventually, though, he became a sort of laughing stock to the rest of the band."

"Brian experimented more with drugs because he didn't care what state he was in the next day for the gig or the studio."

"We'd spend an awful lot of time trying to get through to Brian, trying to help him, but we'd have it flung back in our faces. We were working night after night. If someone isn't pulling their weight after a while it becomes incredibly difficult."

"Brian wanted to be a pop star the minute he saw The Beatles. He
got left behind in the crush and someone asked him for his autograph.
At the time The Beatles had only been around for a couple of months
nationally. And you know how long it takes the public to recognise
faces. Especially at night. Success went to Brian's head immediately.
And the more successful we became the more it interfered with his
compatibility within the band, and the more he thought he was
involved in a competition with me and Mick."

"Brian got really ill in Chicago and we did the whole Midwest
without him. Brian was in hospital and we had to go on through all
these hick towns like St Louis, Dayton and Cleveland. It was a lot of
work for me at the time, but there were still a lot of teenyboppers so
nobody could hear anyway. At that time screaming was taken for
granted. I tried to play the most important part of each song instead
of just doing my bit. If Brian's part of a particular song was most
important then I would do his part and forget mine."

"The main thing that pissed us off with Brian was he didn't pull
his weight with the band. He insisted playing his pop star bullshit.
It wasn't just himself he was fuckin' about. He was fuckin' the band
about as well. When we were working without any breaks we were
considerate to Brian. But there came a time where one had to be
absolutely shitty to Brian. But we were not shittier than he had been
to us over a much longer period. No one had the patience or strength
to put up with it any more."

Anita Pallenburg

"As far as I know Brian Jones never wrote a single finished
song in his life; he wrote bits and pieces but he never presented them
to us. No doubt he spent hours, weeks, working on things, but his
paranoia was so great he could never bring himself to present it to us."
(1974)

"I don't know what Brian would have gone on to do, quite honestly.
Even though he was talking about getting a new band together and
doing it all again, I don't think that's what he would have ended up
doing if he had lived. I think he might have gone into movie music, or
maybe something entirely different, collecting butterflies or something.
But I don't think he was leaving the Stones just to start it all over again
with some other band." (1973)

"I don't know what Brian resented. I think Brian resented everything.
By that period Brian's main preoccupation was a severe paranoia about
being busted. He had no other thoughts in his head except hiding from
the police. Consequently that made him think less and less about what
he really should be doing, which was making music."

"There was extra hassles between Brian and myself because I took his
old lady. You know, he enjoyed beating chicks up. Not a likeable guy.

At the same time he had a certain charm. And we all tried at certain times to get on with him but then he'd shit on you. It sounds like I'm just putting him down but I want to tell the truth about this. You ask anyone else in the Stones and if they're honest they'll say the same thing.

"He wanted to be the boss man. The first time that dawned on me was very early days when we were playing in Liverpool, the Cavern actually, and we found out that he'd persuaded the powers that be that he should be taking five quid a week extra. He used to get in all sorts of trouble and expect you to get him out of it. Everybody went through periods of trying to get along with him. But you're working and travelling every day and you just don't have time to take care of this… fragile monster." (1988)

"He contributed in other ways, like the different colours that he added by playing around with other instruments. He had an incredible talent for walking into a studio and, whatever was lying around, he may never have touched that instrument in his life before, but by the time the song was halfway there, he'd have a riff down, like a sitar on 'Paint It Black', sometimes chimes and marimbas, all these kind of things. So he contributed a lot in making The Rolling Stones' records sometimes have these extra exotic colours going on in the tapestry, in the weave, the warp and the weft." (1988)

His death

"There was no-one there that would want to murder (Brian). Somebody didn't take care of him. And they should have done, because he had somebody there who was supposed to take care of him… Everyone knew what Brian was like, especially at a party. Maybe he did just go in for a swim and have an asthma attack. I never saw Brian have an attack although I knew he was asthmatic. He was a good swimmer. He was a better swimmer than anybody else around me. He could dive off rocks straight into the sea. He was really easing back from the drugs thing. He wasn't hitting them like he had been, he wasn't hitting anything like he had. Maybe the combination of things, it's one of those things I just can't find out. We were completely shocked. He was a goddamn good swimmer and it's just very hard to believe he could have died in a swimming pool… It's the same feeling with who killed Kennedy. You can't go to the bottom of it." (1971)

"(Brian's death) was a complete shock. I always knew Brian was a very fragile person. When I think about it, there are certain people you meet - and Brian was probably one of them - who you couldn't imagine getting old. He's one of those people that you know are going to go fairly young, because they burn it all up so quick. Nevertheless, that didn't lessen the shock when it happened. Being with that cat for seven or eight years non-stop, you know, to have him suddenly removed completely, it really knocked us back.

"There was just a feeling amongst us that we just had to get on with it, and the best way was just to do it as soon as possible, and show everybody that the rest of us were still alive and kicking. That's probably the best thing we could have done." (1973)

"I don't think honestly you'll find anyone who liked Brian (Jones). Brian was not a likeable guy. He had so many hang-ups, he was unreliable, he wanted to be a star. I admired his grit and determination... Listen, I'm being honest, right? I could say, oh yeah, Brian, lovely guy. But I'm being honest and he had so many hang-ups he didn't know where to hang himself. So he drowned himself.

"So, no, I wasn't surprised about Brian. I didn't wish him dead and there are a few guys who did, but in all honesty it was no surprise. He was out there and I really don't think he ever expected to live. Brian was the one who said, 'I'll never make 30'. Of course his parents are going to read this and it's a terrible thing to say, in a way. But I'm just saying what I really think. I'm sorry." (1988)

MICK TAYLOR

"The band is still improving, it's still getting better. I still feel there's more to come from it, and probably a lot of that's due to Mick (Taylor). A bit of new blood in there is always a good thing. He contributes a lot, in the studio, in the construction of records, he's getting to know a lot more about recording now, something he hasn't done until this point. He's OK." (1973)

"I was very impressed with Mick Taylor. He is a great guitar player. I always got on well with him. In the early days I wasn't as close to him because Mick Taylor is a very reserved guy."

"Both the horns and Mick Taylor made their début on the same album on the same track. At the time a lot of people overlooked the fact that it wasn't just Mick joining the band, that was the whole period where the horns joined too. And they all left at the same time."

"This band is less slick and sophisticated sounding than the other one at its best when everybody was in tune and could hear each other. This is a lot funkier, dirtier and rougher and a lot more exciting. The problem for us when Mick Taylor left was whether to replace him or take the opportunity of a break to form a new band and make it different. Mick was a really nice player, but his interest was in melody and harmony and notes." (1975)

"The Stones ain't gonna end just because a guitar player dies or leaves. We crossed the problem of Brian's death so successfully that it's actually harder to cross this one because Mick Taylor dropped in so successfully."

BILL

"One of the things about people is that they don't change that much. Bill is pretty much the same as he's always been. He's a different thing in England, I hear. A bit of a TV celeb. I always told him he'd get in trouble with those young chicks. He's always been a bastard for that though. He didn't believe that he was ever gonna be in a position where chicks would be falling over to get to a Rolling Stone so he took full advantage of that. But I think the older he gets the younger they get. Which, as I said, is gonna become a *prahblem*. Apart from that he hasn't changed much." (1988)

"Now, if we did go on tour without Bill, I'm sure he'll be very pissed off and that's what I'm counting on. But then, Bill's from a different generation. For him, success is going on *The Michael Aspel Show*. I think he's on his third menopause; certainly can't be his first!" (1991)

"Bill, though… he's another matter. I've got to see Bill eyeball to eyeball to get this thing sorted out once and for all.

"I don't want to say too much, but I don't want to see this line-up change now. Bill's reasons - I don't know if he knows what they are, I've gotta find out. My basic attitude is the Stones are getting tougher and I expect him to be there but at the same time I know I can't leave it that long. I don't wanna hear any more rumours and bullshit. It won't stop the Stones going on, though I don't know what we'd do. Maybe he's happy running his restaurants and marrying people he never sees again. I don't know.

"Bill's this very noncommittal guy, which is why I can't talk to him on the phone. Charlie said maybe we could threaten to replace him with a chick - maybe that will do the trick!" (1992)

CHARLIE

"It's Charlie Watts' band - without him we wouldn't have a group." (1986)

"Charlie Watts is my absolute favourite. He has all of the qualities that I like in people. Great sense of humour, a lovely streak of eccentricity, a real talent, very modest. The only thing about Charlie that's always been true is that he's always hated being a pop star. He genuinely loathes it. It's not the image that he wanted. He wanted to be a kind of Max Roach hipster - a cool guy. He suddenly got thrown into this thing that was really not part of his self image." (1988)

"God forbid they should ever get around to making a Stones movie! I certainly wouldn't want to watch it. I hope I'm dead and gone by then. Never mind Mick and I. Who'd play Charlie?" (1991)

RONNIE

"Ronnie Wood has a spirit and feel which is perfectly suitable for the Stones. Even though he's the new boy, he's done his job longer than Brian and Mick. To me, he's the perfect guitar player." (1988)

"Ronnie lives near us in New York. He comes round to me or I go to see him if the old lady locks me out." (1987)

"Ronnie's a great mixture of talent and bullshit. He's the person I communicate with most within the Stones. He called me about getting up with the Midget, Prince, the other night. He fucked up the ending of 'Miss You'? Yeah, that's Ron. But he's a great family man and I admire that. I do love Ronald." (1988)

ANDREW OLDHAM (Manager/producer)

"Andrew (Oldham) had the same naïve experience or lack of experience that we had. In the studio when we made our first records he had absolutely no experience. Andrew didn't know what the fuck he was doing nor did we. We just learned as we went along. He relied on our experience of playing clubs for two years."

IAN 'STU' STEWART

"Stu was unique from the first day I met him. He'd wear these ludicrous black leather shorts and always ride a bike. When we rehearsed at the Bricklayer's Arms, Stu would always be looking out the window to make sure his bike was still there.

"He'd keep one eye on the bike and one eye on the piano. And he'd always hit the right notes. At night the women of the street would appear and Stu would always say something like, 'Whoa, I'd love to wrap myself around that!' And he'd never miss a note."

"I wanted to keep The Rolling Stones together whatever and I believed I could do it… Mr Bravado. But when Ian Stewart died the glue fell out: that was the final thing, and I realised we'd better take some time to rethink everything." (1988)

SIDEMEN

"The problem which I was ignorant of for a long time was studio musicians and sidemen taking over the band. The real problem with those albums was the band was led astray by brilliant players like Billy Preston. We'd start off a typical Stones track and Billy would start playin' something so fuckin' good musically that we'd get sidetracked and end up with a compromised track. That made a difference."

The Music

'Come On' (First single, 1963)

"When we released our very first single, 'Come On', we were doing gigs every night and we refused to play it. How could we go out and do our set of heavy rhythm and blues and then play this little pop song? It was too embarrassing, man." (1989)

    "As a first record we knew that something like 'Come On' was needed to start with. We had no intention of that leading the way to what we were going to do next. We did 'Come On' because it was the most commercial sound we were capable of making at the time. And the song had some kind of affinity with what we were used to doing."

'The Rolling Stones' (First album, 1964)

"The entire record ('The Rolling Stones') was virtually our
stage act apart from one or two dubs thrown in. 80 per cent of it
was straight what we played at Studio 51 or Richmond."

"When we were recording our first album, two track was 'it'.
Now everything sounds so clean and sanitised, like a supermarket,
all hygienically wrapped." (1974)

"We did it on a two-track Revox in a room insulated with egg
cartons at Regent Sound. Under those primitive conditions it was easy
to make that kind of sound but hard to make a much better one."
(1978)

'(I Can't Get No) Satisfaction' (Single, 1965)

"I was in a hotel with a little cassette recorder next to me. I pushed
the button and I got the guitar and I sort of ran through the sequence
once - and on the tape you can hear me drop the pick and the rest
of the tape is me snoring. The next morning I listened to the tape.

It was about two minutes of acoustic guitar and a very rough riff of 'Satisfaction' and then me snoring for forty minutes." (1986)

"'Satisfaction' is probably the only number which we feel has been better interpreted by another artist - we preferred Otis Redding's version to our own... Mick usually writes the lyrics and I write the music. You just get an idea - a phrase like 'I can't get no satisfaction' or 'Get off of my cloud' and you build from it. One leads to another." (1974)

"The Stones got so big after 'Satisfaction' that we would work for several months frantically recording, and then have eighteen months sometimes in which we'd do absolutely nothing! You wouldn't even see the guys!" (1989)

"We very rarely play 'Satisfaction' live. We only ever did it if we had to. It's bizarre. It's the biggest record we've ever had and if we can get away with it we won't play it. But we've got a good version going this time. Got the rhythm right. Fuzztone, bye bye. I'll tell you, I never did like that record. I nicked the riff... but I never did like gimmicks and I was tied to this little Fuzztone box. D'you know that was written because we needed another track for the album and we knocked it out to fill the album up? I thought there was something there when the guys in the control room started jumping up and down going, it's the single! It's the single!" (1989)

'Get Off Of My Cloud' (Single, 1965)

"I never dug it as a record. The chorus was a nice idea, but we rushed it out as a follow-up to 'Satisfaction'. We were in LA, and it was time for another single. Actually, what I wanted was to do it slow like a Lee Dorsey thing. We rocked it up. I thought it was one of Andrew's worse productions." (1971)

'I'm Free' (US B-side of 'Get Off Of My Cloud', 1965)

"Nobody's ever totally free, and free from what? I think a lot of people don't even know what's holding them captive. Sometimes it's themselves." (1991)

'Under My Thumb' (1966, on 'Aftermath')

"It was a spin-off from our environment: hotels, and too many dumb chicks. Not all dumb, not by any means, but that's how one got."

'Lady Jane' (1966, on 'Aftermath')

"Brian was getting into dulcimer then, because he dug Richard Farina. To me, 'Lady Jane' is very Elizabethan. There are a few places in England where people still speak that way, Chaucer English."

**'Goin' Home'
(1966, on 'Aftermath')**

"It was the first long rock'n'roll cut. It broke that two-minute barrier. We tried to make singles as long as we could do then because we just liked to let things roll on. The song was written in just the first two and a half minutes: we just happened to keep the tape rolling, me on guitar, Brian on harp, Bill and Charlie and Mick. If there's a piano, it's Stu." (1971)

'Paint It Black' (Single, 1966)

"Mick wrote it. I wrote the music, he did the words. Get a single together. What's amazing about that one for me is the sitar. Also, the fact that we cut it as a comedy track. Bill was playing organ, doing a take-off of our first manager who started his career in show business as an organist in a cinema pit. We'd been doing it with funky rhythms and it hadn't worked, and he started playing like this and everybody got behind it. It's a two-beat, very strange. Brian playing the sitar makes it a whole other thing.

"There were some weird letters, racial letters. 'Was there a comma in the title? Was this an order to the world?'"

**'Have You Seen Your Mother Baby,
Standing In The Shadow' (Single, 1966)**

"With 'Have You Seen Your Mother?' we were starting to change directions slightly. We just didn't have the physical energy to attempt that. We'd been on the road for four non-stop years."

**'Let's Spend The Night Together'
(Single, 1967)**

"That song really came as a spin-off of 'Have You Seen Your Mother Baby'. I could only play one or two on the piano, especially way back then. I'm maybe a little more accomplished now - to me it's just a way of getting out of always using one instrument to write." (1986)

'Between The Buttons' (1967)

"'Between The Buttons' was the last album we did before we stopped working. As far as we were concerned it was still part of the period we'd been living; that same pattern of touring America two or three times a year, going to RCA to record."

"It was the last album we made with everyone in the band well oiled and ready to go, straight off the road." (1989)

'Their Satanic Majesties Request' (1967)

"'Satanic Majesties' was really almost done semi-comatose, sort of, 'Do we really have to make an album?' 'Yeah.'" (1988)

"It was so weird to make an album and not be on the road that it was totally unlike recording. I liked a few songs like '2,000 Light Years', 'Citadel' and 'She's A Rainbow', but basically I thought the ('Satanic Majesties') album was a load of crap. That album was made under the pressure of the court case and the whole scene that was going on in London at the time."

'Street Fighting Man' (Single, 1968)

"The first time I really realised the value of acoustic instruments was on 'Street Fighting Man', when the only electric instrument on there is the bass, which I overdubbed afterwards. Otherwise all those guitars are acoustics." (1988)

"That's been interpreted thousands of different ways because it really is ambiguous as a song. Trying to be revolutionary in Grosvenor Square. Mick went to all those demonstrations and got charged by the cops." (1971)

'Jumping Jack Flash' (Single, 1968)

The feeling's one of exhilaration: as soon as I pick up the guitar and play that riff, something happens here - in your stomach. It's one of the better feelings in the world: you just jump on the riff and it plays you. Matter of fact it takes you over. It's an amazing, superhuman feeling. An explosion would be the best way to describe it. It's the one that I would immediately go to if I wanted to approach the state of nirvana." (1991)

'Beggars Banquet' (1968)

"This was a very special album. It was fun to make, and it got more and more exciting as each track built up, and I did realise that we were getting the essence of the Stones down on tape. But each song individually? No, you're so involved in the actual mechanics - 'Oh, you mean it goes to *this* chord instead of... Oh, right' - you're so close to it, that you don't think about it with every song. It's more that the whole collection of songs starts to impress you in that way." (1988)

"There was no immediate necessity to go through the drama of replacing Brian because no gigs were lined up. We first had to recognise the fact that we needed to make a really good album. After 'Satanic Majesties' we wanted to make a Stones album."

"As far as the album was shaping up as we were making it, I had a definite feeling that we were starting to find The Rolling Stones in there." (1988)

"'Beggars Banquet' was the first record on which I was fooling around with different tunings."

'No Expectations' (1968, on 'Beggars Banquet')

"I wrote it real quick, just sitting around at home, and then when I took it into the studio, Brian put that lovely slide guitar on. I just remember it being such a lovely song, and it was so easy to make. You didn't have to put a lot of work into it. The song almost wrote itself." (1988)

'Dear Doctor' (1968, on 'Beggars Banquet')

"It was almost a joke, because of the tempo of it and the rhythm. 'Dear Doctor' was really almost a booze-up, just cutting the track and just having a laugh. It was just fun to make, that one, just crashing away. 'Dear Doctor, please help me...' Once you'd started, everybody started yelling out lines. It just buzzed by. A load of fun, and I think just one or two takes, probably." (1988)

'Prodigal Son' (1968, on 'Beggars Banquet')

"I had quite a lot of time off just before and it was the first time for quite a while that I'd actually had time to sit around and listen to all my old blues records. And first off I loved the idea of this song, I loved the biblical quality in the subject matter." (1988)

'Factory Girl' (1968, on 'Beggars Banquet')

"'Factory Girl' basically came from me tinkling around with a little
bit of, not so much blue-grass music, but early white hillbilly music.
And since I was working very much with acoustic guitars on this
album, I was playing it a lot and I was getting my finger-picking down
a little bit, and Nicky (Hopkins) came up with that fiddle effect.

"Mick wrote most of the lyrics to that. It's basically his idea,
lyrically, and it was just my little finger-picking riff behind it." (1988)

'Parachute Woman' (1968, on 'Beggars Banquet')

"It was another cassette job, and we just thought it was such a funny
idea - 'Parachute woman, land on me tonight'. It was maybe just a few
takes. I cranked it out on a cassette player, and then buzzed it through
an extension speaker with a microphone in front of it, and then we put
it onto an eight-track. We probably put that one down in two or three
goes." (1988)

'Stray Cat Blues' (1968, on 'Beggars Banquet')

"It was just like a real good, heavy blues riff. It always reminded me
a bit of Albert King in a way, not the style of playing or anything, but
just that tempo and that dark kind of riff, and probably came out of
playing in the States for three or four years and working with guys like
that and listening to that stuff on the radio all the time." (1988)

'Salt Of The Earth' (1968, on 'Beggars Banquet')

"It was just an attempt to switch the lead vocal sound and give it
a different sound, and it would maybe make people just listen to it in
a different way, take a little more notice of it, rather than just the lead
vocalist doing his thing.

"When I was putting the track down, I was singing, and Mick was
listening to how it was being put together… Mick got into it, and so
we just used the best that we'd got."

'Sympathy For The Devil' (1968, on 'Beggars Banquet')

"When we were just innocent kids out for a good time, they're
saying, 'They're evil, they're evil.' Oh, I'm evil, really? So that makes
you start thinking about evil…

"It's something everybody should explore. There are possibilities
there. A lot of people have played on it, and it's inside everybody.
I mean. Doctor John's whole trip is based on it."

'Let It Bleed' (1969)

"I would hate to pull one out from 'Beggars Banquet', 'Let It Bleed', 'Sticky Fingers' and 'Exile On Main Street'. We really hit a consistent stride there. And if it tailed off a little bit after that, I think that was not so much to do with being the Seventies rich jet-set-superstar-rock-and-roll-whatever, but more to do with the fact that, in order to keep the band together, we'd had to leave England. So I couldn't just call Mick up and say, 'I'll be over in ten minutes - I've got a great idea for a song'."

'Honky Tonk Women' (1969)

"I wrote it as a real Hank Williams/Jimmie Rodgers/Thirties country song and it got turned round to this other thing by Mick Taylor who got into a completely different feel throwing it off the wall another way."

'Sticky Fingers' (1971)

"I don't think 'Sticky Fingers' is a heavy drug album any more than the world is a heavy world… I mean you can't take a fucking record like other people take a Bible. It's only a fucking record, man." (1971)

'Wild Horses' (1971, on 'Sticky Fingers')

"We wrote the chorus in the john of the Muscle Shoals recording studio because it didn't finish off right. It was about Marlon's birth, 'cause I knew we were going to have to go to America and start work again… and not really wanting to go away. It was a very delicate moment: the kid's only two months old and you're goin' away. Millions of people do it all the time, but still…" (1971)

'Exile On Main Street' (1972)

"The fact is that Mick spent most of his time during 'Exile' away, 'cause Bianca was pregnant; ya know, royalty is having a baby. So what am I supposed to do? I'm supposed to be making an album. But I never considered it my album."

"I did 'Exile On Main Street' when I was heaviest into smack and that was a fuckin' double album. Personally I don't think it affected my productivity at all. You really can't say smack contributed to me not being able to function anywhere. I even got skiing together when I was a junkie. I wonder how many people have done that?"

"Suddenly for 'Exile' we all left England and went to France and recorded that in my house – and after that slowly everybody dispersed to different parts of the globe, so the lull in that period was more to do with just the geographical difficulties of getting it together. The boys weren't just around the corner, living on top of each other, as we had always done before, and I think it had something more to do with that, just the difficulties of keeping it together, that made it harder to make good records, yeah." (1988)

'Happy' (1972, on 'Exile On Main Street')

"The basic track was Bobby Keys on baritone sax, myself on guitar and Jimmy Miller on drums. 'Happy' was cut one afternoon because the whole record was cut in the basement of my villa with the Stones mobile truck parked in the driveway. So sometimes I would be ready to play and some of the guys would come over early. It was really like a warm-up, but had this idea for a song."

'Goat's Head Soup' (1973)

"'Goat's Head Soup' to me was a marking-time album. I like it in many ways but I don't think it has the freshness that 'It's Only Rock'n'Roll' has… Rock'n'roll can't be planned or prepared. You can have a few basic structures though. I'm not the sort of person who sits down at home with a guitar, writes a song and says, 'That's how I hear it,' because I play in a band and leave it up to them to tell me how it should go for them." (1974)

"It didn't turn out like we wanted it to – not blaming (producer) Jimmy Miller or anything like that, because there's no-one to blame. But it was obvious that it was time for a change in that particular part of the process of making records." (1974)

'Star Star' (1973, on 'Goat's Head Soup')

"They've given us a lot of trouble for all the wrong reason. They even got down to saying that Steve McQueen would pass an injunction against the song because of the line about him. So we just sent a tape of the song to him, and of course he okayed it. It was just a hassle though… obstacles put in our way."

'It's Only Rock'n'Roll' (1974)

"Right, well first off we had to put that particular track ('It's Only Rock'n'Roll') out as a single. In all honesty… well you probably know the story already… the track itself was originally recorded at Ronnie Wood's place with Mick, Ronnie and Kenny Jones.

"Anyway Mick took the track down to Munich and when I heard it I thought great y'know… I just felt that it said what it had to say very well, what with everybody running around trying to write the definitive rock'n'roll song. It was put very simply and directly. So we immediately set about re-recording it but the problem was that Kenny Jones in fact had done a great take-off of Charlie's drumming which, for that number, even surpassed Charlie himself. So Charlie had to do a take-off of Kenny Jones doing a take-off of him and ended up so paranoid about it that I decided to leave the original track on. We ended up constructing the whole song around Kenny's sessions.

"I'm just playing the Superfly 'wah-wah' stuff. Mick (Jagger)'s playing the rhythm guitar. He's so good now it almost frightens me. Yeah… Mick T on bass, Bill on synthesiser - that low growling sound. Actually we were lucky in that during the sessions we got hold of that machine, it looks like those bathroom scales… I think it's called a 'Hi-Fli' and it gets all these great sounds out of the guitars. The real battle these days y'see is to keep the raw quality - that raunchy sound you can get naturally from a decent guitar and keep it on the tape itself throughout the whole mixing process. I mean all that shit with 'Dolbys' and what-have-you. Those things just sterilise the good gritty rock'n'roll sound right out of existence." (1974)

'Luxury' (1974, on 'It's Only Rock'n'Roll')

"Yeah, well first off, that *is* a bona fide reggae 'on-beat' being played there ('Luxury'), no matter what anyone may tell you. The song's mine basically. It all came about while I was driving from the Munich Hilton to the studios, fucked right out of my head and the radio was playing this soul number which I still don't know the title of but it had this chord sequence… and it turned out later as 'Luxury'. I just played it as a straight rock'n'roll thing until Charlie turned the beat around and it all fell spontaneously into place with Mick getting into that whole West Indian bit etc. That really is a prime typical Stones track in the way that it fell together by accident. I mean, that's how you get influenced. It's a process of slow assimilation." (1974)

'Black And Blue' (1976)

"Rehearsing guitar players, that's what that one was about." (1976)

'Some Girls' (1978)

"Mick is a frustrated musician. He played a lot of guitar on 'Some Girls' and he didn't play badly. He turns his amp up so loud you can't

distinguish what he plays. But he's so intensely trying to be in the band to the point of playing guitar on everything."

"Mick feels the need to get into other caricatures. He's slightly vaudeville in his approach. 'Faraway Eyes' is like that. He did it great every time except for the final take. It's good when he does it straight 'cause it's funny enough without doing a pantomime. It's the sound version of what he was doing wrong visually. When he sings it as a caricature it sounds like it would be great for a show. You expect Mick to walk out in his cowboy duds on an 18-wheeler set. Or sing it into his CB as part of his skit."

"I think 'Some Girls' was the most immediate album we had done in a long while, and you can't argue with seven million sales!" (1979)

'Miss You' (Single, 1978)

A lot of our songs take a long while to come out. But it still comes together even when Mick and I haven't seen each other for months. We help each other on songs like 'Miss You', which came together during the 1976 tour of Europe." (1979)

'Dance' (1980, on 'Emotional Rescue')

"I saw 'Dance' as more of an instrumental, like Junior Walker's 'Shotgun', and Mick immediately came up with *reams* of paper and lyrics. I thought it should be a minimal lyric, and Mick comes up with *Don Giovanni*."

'Start Me Up' (Single, 1981)

"That was in the can for ages, and mostly we'd forgotten about it. We had about thirty takes of it reggae, and there was just one or two other takes where we did it with a backbeat, just straight rock'n'roll. So to us it was that interminable reggae track we did way back when. And then - right at the end of the reel - was this rock'n'roll version, you know."

'Dirty Work' (1987)

"With 'Dirty Work', I built that to go on the road. It was like 'Some Girls'. Deliberately structured so that every song could be played live, simply, easy. Then we finished the record and Mick suddenly said 'I ain't gahn on nah fakkin' rawd'. So that was the plug pulled from under me." (1988)

"Mick was already involved with his solo work and wasn't there
very much. Charlie was going through a weird period, which he does
from time to time. Very rarely do all these things coincide: they never
coincided before. So Ronnie played drums on 'Sleep Tonight' and
I wrote it on piano. I love the changes on it. I realised I was getting
into another area that I hadn't expected for myself, and to me it was,
in a way, an indication of what could be done on 'Talk Is Cheap'."
(1989)

'Steel Wheels' (1989)

"This one reminds me of making 'Exile On Main Street'... the
willingness, that everybody's into it. Everybody went to France to
make 'Exile', we were very determined we were going to keep the
band together in spite of all that. There's a bit of that atmosphere here
too, to prove something. There's nothing like it. These guys work
best under pressure." (1989)

"Maybe what I need out of this one is to prove that the Stones are
still a great band, that there's still plenty more in there, that it's not just
a rehash or leaning on our past... that it's still alive and kicking."
(1989)

'Highwire' (Single, 1991)

"We were in the studio working on the track when the news came
on the TV that the Gulf War had started.
     "It's not about the war *per se* – the war was over by the time it hit
the shops. Basically, it's about how such things start in the first place.
You get various governments building up the army of some tin-pot
dictator like Saddam Hussein and letting him get away with murder for
years. Many of those same companies were still actively trading with
him when the UN were delivering their ultimatum. He's probably still
wondering what he did wrong!
     "So, the only time you can bring out a record like 'Highwire'
is while the heat is on, and make people aware of the background to
events. The song's basically Mick's thing, and he did say he thought
we'd draw some fire, but not in Britain – we just expected that any flak
would come from flag wavers, here in America. As is happens, nobody
except that ambitious MP looking to make a name for himself publicly
objected." (1991)

SOLO RECORDS

"If I made a solo album I'd only hire the band to play on it anyway.
So why bother?"

"I love to work and the idea of doing a solo album, to me, has always been No Way because it's always been an admission that I couldn't keep the Stones, my band, together. There's a little bit of that involved. I'm not saying it's like a big *heeaavy* thing but somewhere back there (points to his head) it was there. Also there was the thing of, who the hell am I going to play with after playing with Charlie Watts for 25 years? What am I going to do, you know? Do I feel like fronting the whole goddamn thing? So it took, like, two years to sort all that out.

"Stu (Ian Stewart) died just at that time and very few people realise how important he was to the Stones. He was the glue that held all the bits together. The combination of the two things left me in limbo. Suddenly, it was, what can I do?" (1988)

"I couldn't use any of the Stones: otherwise there would be too many grey areas." (1988)

"That (the Ex-Pensive Winos)'s the unofficial name of the band. The reason they're called that is I caught three of 'em behind the drum kit doing a bottle of Lafitte Rothschild one night, in a break. I said, put that down, winos! And they said, it's Lafitte Rothschild, man, we're *expensive* winos! So later we figured we'd give it a little kick and make it Ex-Pensive. It's all clever stuff!" (1988)

'Talk Is Cheap'

"I'm quite proud of it: I still actually like to listen to it." (1989)

"I have more exact, more perfect or skilful takes of each of these songs, but the more you try to literally perfect them the more you lose the instinctive thing. Instinct is what I want." (1989)

"It was great because Bootsy (Collins) used to work with James Brown and the horn player on the track, Maceo Parker, runs James Brown's band. So it was a little hats off to James Brown. There are a lot of little tributes on this album. Hats off coming here and there. There's even a little one to, bless their souls, the Fab Four. That's on 'Whip It Up'. It's a deliberate early Beatles way of doing things on the harmony vocals. We recorded the whole thing basically like we would with the Stones with everyone playing live in the studio which apparently now is a novelty. I don't know why. To me that's one of the most essential things about making a rock'n'roll record. It has to be spontaneous with lots of room-sound, ambience. Let the sound buzz around the room instead of tightening it up and keeping everyone sounding clear and clean and in a box. To me as a musician, your canvas is silence and what you do is fuck around with silence. Same with a painting, you are confronted with a rectangular empty space and you splash paint all over it." (1988)

Songwriting

First efforts

"Writing... I suppose really the credit for that must go to Andrew (Oldham, the Stones' manager), because I'd never thought of writing. It had never occurred to me. I thought that was something else, like being a novelist or a computer operator. It was a completely different field, that I hadn't thought of. I just thought of myself as a guitar player. It hadn't occurred to Mick either. Although I suppose we dabbled with it occasionally, when we were sitting around with Brian, but I remember we just gave up in despair.

"It was Andrew who really forced Mick and I to sit down and try it, and who got us through that initial period that you have to go through where you just write absolute rubbish. You just rewrite other people's songs. Until you start coming up with songs of your own. It was Andrew that made us persevere with that. Maybe because he wanted to promote the group, and get as much out of us as possible, I suppose." (1973)

"Mick and I being songwriters affected Brian a lot. It took Brian a long time to come to terms with that 'cause it was very early on. After that he never regained any sort of status. He lost more and more interest as he went along. It got to the point where we were going into the studio and Brian had to play or learn a song that Mick and I had written. That would bring him down more and more."

"One could say, really generally, that I've written more of the music and Mick's written more of the lyrics. But it's never that cut and dried, even within one song." (1986)

"I can't walk into the studio with a song with words typed out on a sheet of paper and say this is it, this is how it goes, play it. I might as well hire session men then. I just go in there with a germ of an idea. The smaller the germ the better, and I give it to them, feed it to them and see what they do with it. Then it comes out like a Rolling Stones record, instead of me telling everyone what I want they can work it out any way they want from that point."

"When you're writing for somebody like the Stones, unless there's a conscious change, like there was in '67, when everyone wanted to do different things and try out things – unless there's a conscious effort, there's the same approach still. You write songs which you know the band are going to be really able to get their teeth into." (1973)

"I generally sit down and just write continuously until I come to the end of a progression of ideas. I seldom come back to something.

It's a strange thing, but I always get the biggest kick out of the anticipation of a song. It's the knowledge of having written something which might be our next single which is the real kick. By the time it's out on the market I've forgotten it and we're generally writing the next one." (1974)

"You don't create songs. They're not all your creation. You just sort of pluck them out of the air, if you're around and receptive, and then you say, 'I kind of like this,' and something about the songs says, 'I'm worth the time and the trouble to keep playing me and find out.' And if you hang on to their tail long enough, suddenly you get, 'Ah, there I am, I'm ready.' So you have to listen to the mechanics of the song all the time, and be very receptive to what it's trying to tell you while you're making it." (1988)

"I still don't care, about going into the studio with half a song, because I know that what's going to be played and what's going to go down in the studio is going to help you finish it off." (1988)

"Once I started writing songs - I think with Mick too - it was a pleasure. It's fun to write songs, and I've never had a writer's block. The main trouble I have with songs is which ones to cut out. The amount of stuff that's recorded, for the number of tracks that you actually get on an album, you have just the tip of the iceberg usually, and so you end up working on the ones you feel are most advanced in their development. There are some you say, 'I love this song, but it's going to take a lot of work,' and 'That one needs to go back in the barrel and ferment for a while,' so you save it. And you tend to go for the ones that you feel are most advanced and that the band have got the essence of to the degree that you want it. So a lot depends on that. At least it's better than not having enough songs." (1988)

"Sometimes you write songs while you're making one record, tinkling around in between takes, and you say, 'Oh, just cut that on two-track and save it for later', so other songs are being written while you're making a record…
   "If an idea comes up, you go, 'Hold it a minute, man, I just want to put this idea down for later'. So you get a lot of bits and pieces left over that would come off on the next album. You'd work like that. Never with the Stones, or on any session that I've ever done, has somebody walked in with a typewritten sheet of paper and said, 'Well, it goes like this,' because even if you tried it, it wouldn't go like that by the time you finished." (1988)

Marianne Faithfull

"I don't think that rock'n'roll songwriters should worry about Art.
I don't think it comes into it. A lot of it is just craft anyway, especially
after doing it for a long time… As far as I'm concerned, Art is just
short for Arthur." (1986)

Writing for others

"To me, and to Mick at the same time, writing a song was as
different as someone who makes a saddle for a horse and someone who
puts the shoes on it. It's a different gig. I play 'em, you write 'em.
We explained this to Andrew (Oldham) and he just locked us in a
kitchen for a day and said, when you come out, make sure you come
out with a song. So we sat down and wrote 'As Tears Go By' which
went on to be a Number 1 when Marianne Faithfull sang it.
So we thought, yeah, it can be done. 'Cos at the time that was the sort
of song we'd never play. We were trying to write 'Hoochie Coochie
Man' and you come out with a song that's almost like 'Greensleeves'!
But, it gives you the confidence to think, well if we can write one, we
can write two." (1988)

"I can imagine (writing for other people), yes. I can do it. I wouldn't
think it would be that much of an effort to write for somebody else.
It would just require the time that I put into the Stones. But it takes
up most of the time, really, to write enough material, enough Stones
fodder for a year. But if things change, I've no doubt I could write
for - the Queen Mother if I had to." (1973)

"When we heard Aretha Franklin's version of 'Satisfaction',
suddenly Mick and I thought we were actually songwriters! I've
always been chuffed that anyone would want to do versions of our
stuff. It's a great compliment. And it's always interesting to hear new
variations. Yeah, even the Devo and Residents ones." (1992)

Concerts

HIGHS AND LOWS

High: Hyde Park, July 1969

"You'll never see Hyde Park like that – just people and trees.
But it was a hassle quite honestly. It was fantastic from the point
of view of a mass gathering. But Brian had died and we were just
breaking in Mick Taylor. We hadn't played live for quite a while and
the organisation, the logistical end of it was flimsy. No-one really
knew what was going on, the sound was terrible. Some of the
highlights of my life are the gigs where no-one can remember where
they were but as you walk off the stage you look at each other and say
that maybe, tonight, we *were* the best rock'n'roll band in the world.
That marvellous feeling when you go beyond your expectations of
perfection." (1988)

Low: Altamont, December 1969

"I wouldn't say frightening but definitely high in adrenaline
wondering who the hell was running the joint. Five hundred thousand
people, guys getting stabbed, the Hell's Angels are out of it on acid
and bad wine – Thunderbird! The only way they could cool it was by
facing them down. The one thing you can't do in a situation like that
is to give way to fear or intimidation. The other memory of that is the
actual getaway. Everyone running up this hill to a hovering helicopter.
It was like Vietnam. You had to jump and climb up this rope ladder.
Gotta get away. Trying to make sure you got the women on there
first." (1988)

"One thing Altamont taught us was not to try to do anything like that again. In any case, rock sounds better in a room with two hundred people. It really does."

High: Live Aid, July 1985

"I had no intention of going near it (Live Aid). I don't trust big deal charity gigs. The Stones were asked to play it as a band but they weren't a band any more anyway. They'd already broken up. The reason I did it was because Bob (Dylan) turned up at Ronnie Wood's place and we had some amazing rehearsals. The fact is that to go on at the time we did, just before the end, with three acoustic guitars, at a climax point, is madness. And not having worked together on stage before we didn't know what to expect. I still really enjoyed it, you know, strings were breaking and Bob's a nervous guy and he's looking around, worrying. And there were guys just off stage tuning up electric guitars for the big finale and that's all we could hear so we were playing absolutely deaf. But I enjoyed the fact that it was completely off the cuff." (1988)

Touring with The Stones

"When you play onstage you're so conscious of it that you try to forget and just concentrate on playing. You try to ignore the audience as much as possible. If you think too much about the audience you will just dry up and paralyse yourself."

"My one worry is falling over on stage. This may sound absurd, but I actually slipped on a hamburger in Hamburg once, and almost fell off stage." (1978)

"I'm always pissed off if we're supposed to tour and we don't. We've begun touring less which is stupid."

"You see, with the Stones, it's difficult, because a tour takes months to line up now. Sure I'd like to be able to call up the guys one morning, and say 'Let's play tonight', because that's how it grabs you sometimes. But you can't do that. Setting up gigs these days is a big operation - security and all this shit." (1973)

"When we started this band, we thought we had about two or three years. Now it's a habit, and it's absolutely vital that it works on the road. We need constant contact with a living audience." (1982)

"The fact remains that ever since those far off days in Richmond when we'd have to drive through crowds to play in a club that only held 200, there's never ever been a shortage of audiences when the Stones play live.

  "All we've ever done is to announce that we are to tour and then it's up to the public if they want to come and see us or stay away. Nobody forces anybody to buy tickets, but they do - even more than ever." (1991)

Idols & Contemporaries

Pre-rock

"Mozart is still Mozart and you can't alter the fact that the guy's great." (1988)

ROCK'N'ROLLERS

Elvis Presley

"It's funny. You always know it. Mick and I talked about it a lot. I knew from the minute I first heard Elvis that that's what I wanted to do. Once you've decided that you want to be the best rock'n'roller in the world, you go ahead and try it." (1978)

"At the time, it seemed like there was an avalanche of Elvis stuff, and it was like, 'Who opened the door? Who let these people out?' Because, in England, they seemed to have come from nowhere. At the time, I was just a total outsider, lying back and going, 'Come on, give me some good stuff'. And these were the guys that provided it. You probably never get over your first turn-ons, especially the greats like Presley." (1992)

Little Richard

"'Lucille' is the one that first turned me on, that made me think, rock'n'roll's here. Suddenly, my world went from black and white to Technicolor. It was a bit of a shock, but it was a great one, like, 'Shock me some more!'" (1992)

Robert Johnson

"We never recorded… oh wait a minute we did have this amazing all-night rock'n'roll session once which was a gas. He (Little Richard) even wore his whole Lurex dress and did all his old numbers. I mean, but it's so hard to get 'im to do anything beyond running around screaming 'Shuddup… Shuddup'. Christ, I even had to sit down at the piano myself at one point and bash out 'Miss Ann' missing half the beats until he'd had enough and kicked me off the stool, took over, and everyone went - 'Shooo, thank God for that!'." (1974)

BLUESMEN

Robert Johnson

"He felt pressured and he expressed it very well, an inspiration to us all in how it can be done. I'm not saying it can't be done, but also he's saying 'hot tomatoes, red hot'. He had that, but it wasn't the only thing on his mind, he just had a knack for really expressing that 'hell hound on my trail' thing. He was probably one of *the* examples of how it can be done. But it's very rare to find people who can do that." (1986)

Freddie King

Freddie King

"I would love to have played with Freddie King. I kind of understand the way he died, I kind of recognised in Freddie King a similar spirit, he had too much energy to burn and was trying to calm down after a high and just calmed down too much. But most of the people I've ever wanted to play with, I've played with. When I started playing guitar the idea of playing with Muddy Waters was 'when I get to heaven… if I make it there and he makes it there…' But I actually got to play with him, John Lee, Howlin', Scotty Moore, in a small room, asking him 'How the hell did you do that?'… I actually got to play with them all. You can't ask much more than that from life. And I got paid!" (1992)

Chuck Berry

Chuck Berry

"American musicians are a race apart. The best are just so… obsessive. That's the only word that comes to mind And that statement ties in with someone like Chuck Berry who is the biggest cunt I've ever met. That's *on* the record by the way! He's also the most charming cunt and I've got to like 'im for it all the same even if he is so tight he'll never ever get a half-way decent band together. Like, I did a radio interview with this guy recently who asked me about this statement that Bo Diddley made to the press which claimed that if he'd been white then he'd be just as big as The Rolling Stones. That's crap

Above: Buddy Guy

though, because look, The Jackson 5 are bigger than us right now. It's all a question of ability to adapt." (1974)

"It's a pretty sad indictment on the scene when Berry's biggest hit of all is just a wanker's song! He's always pulled that sort of novelty song bit out at certain junctures in his career. 'Anthony Boy' and… 'Broken Arrow', for example. And yeah, it's feeble but still he is trying to inject a certain amount of humour into rock and God knows, it needs it right now. But I mean then again this is the man who wrote 'Carole'…'Schooldays'…'Let It Rock'." (1974)

"I got involved with Chuck Berry and *Hail! Hail! Rock'n'Roll*, where I found a lot of the band for my solo album. One of the reasons I worked with Chuck Berry was that I felt I owed him so much. When I started I pinched virtually all of his riffs, you know? But I figure I repaid my debt because he was one of the most difficult persons I've ever worked with apart from Mick Jagger. That's why I'm suited to his gig. I thought, if I turn this down I'll have to live with the fact that I chickened out. Because when I started to play the electric guitar, Chuck Berry was my man." (1988)

Junior Wells/Buddy Guy

"It's a fuckin' tragedy when something like what happened when Junior Wells and Buddy Guy supported us on a European tour we did several years ago and were always being booed off, occurs. In a way you've got to take Bo Diddley and Chuck Berry out of that thing though because they did adapt." (1974)

"The way the band fall in with Chuck on ('Back In The USA'), it's just a classic. It rocks. It was either this or 'Johnny B Goode' that made me say, 'Hell, I'd sell my soul to be able to do that'. And I probably did! You never know when the transaction goes down, man. We were always more into playing than any stardom trip. Most of the Stones were sort of anti-fame - 'Oh, that's just too unhip' - but then suddenly we were there, and we had to learn how to make it hip for us." (1992)

Muddy Waters

"When we recorded at the Chess Studios in 1964 Muddy Waters was actually painting the studio when we walked in! There's this guy on top of the ladder wearing a white suit - anybody who wasn't selling records at Chess, they'd have to make themselves useful, it seems. So somebody says, 'Well, meet Muddy Waters,' and we look up and he's standing on a step ladder painting the ceiling. And we're all toppling over ourselves, bewildered, thinking, 'What is this? Is this a hobby of his?'

"Can you imagine? And we're recording in the same studio where he made his records! After that, you start to realise how tough the business can be, here's one of your gods painting the ceiling and you're making a record of some of his songs." (1989)

SIXTIES STARS

Eric Clapton

"Eric used to come and watch us before he could even play. He was one of our fans. The fact that he went away for six months and came back playing better than anybody, made us all sick. But Eric's too much of his own man and he's got his own thing to do. And also I'm not so sure that Eric's such a great team man. I mean, he's Eric Clapton, and he's got such a distinctive style that I think you'd have a clash. He's always said he wanted to and always said he's been pissed off when we've hired somebody else instead of him, but to me it would be like Eric Clapton and The Rolling Stones, rather than The Rolling Stones. I could never see that one working." (1988)

Pete Townshend

"I think Pete's mistake is to consider himself an artist… It's neither here nor there. I don't think you want to call yourself an artist. In show business you are an *ar-tiste*. He left the 'e' off the end. Pete and I are the sort of people who'll argue about that forever… cantankerous son of a bitch." (1986)

Jimi Hendrix

"He was a sweet guy, very similar to me in that he was trying to find his own place to hide. He just hid too deep, that's all. When I got to know him, he was shy and retiring. Thing is, if you want to do good stuff, you're aware that you can't play it safe - you've got to keep pushing the limits. Of course, that can spill over into your life." (1992)

Otis Redding

"It was sad when he died, 'cos it would have been nice to have got together one day. It never occurs to you that somebody's gonna get chopped down that young." (1992)

John Lennon

"John was a great guy, a great writer and a really great spirit. Sometimes I sit at the piano and I find myself playing 'Imagine', and I start reminiscing about John. But, hey, you come and you go. But nobody's forgotten John, Jimi or Otis." (1992)

Bob Dylan

"Dylan is a progressive writer. You only have to listen to 'Blonde On Blonde' and then his early albums to see how far he has gone. People just aren't sympathetic to Bob Dylan. They said that 'Rainy Day Woman' was rubbish, but if you'd been stoned and listened to the disc you would have understood." (1974)

"Bob showed us all in the Sixties a new approach, new ways of writing songs. He came from a folk tradition, which had much looser possibilities, and he showed you that rock'n'roll didn't have to be quite so restricted by that verse-chorus-verse formula. We all pushed each other in those days. Bob's a nasty little bugger. I remember him saying to me, 'I could have written "Satisfaction", Keith, but you couldn't have written "Desolation Row".' I said, 'Well, you're right there, Bob!'" (1992)

Gram Parsons

"Gram blew into town with The Byrds, who were playing Blaises. Gram came back to Mick's Chester Square flat with Roger McGuinn. Their next gig was to be South Africa and we told Gram English bands never ever went there. So he threw in his lot with The Byrds and hung around London."

"Gram was a great friend, gave me an extra area to branch out and explore while I was working with the Stones. There was a time in the mid Sixties where we just came to a halt, and he taught me all about country music - before I was just an outsider, but he showed me the guts, the innards of the music.

"When Gram died it hit me harder than when Brian died. Obviously we had our problems with Brian… but when Gram died he was still on his way up, he still had loads to achieve… so that was much harder to take." (1992)

"There were no ulterior motives for Gram to hang around. And Mick didn't take that into consideration. He basically thought of Gram as just another hanger-on, trying to get as much as possible out of the Stones.

"The reason Gram and I were together more than other musicians is because I really wanted to learn what Gram had to offer. Gram was really intrigued by me and by the band. Although we came from England, Gram and I shared this instinctive affinity for the real South."

Phil Spector

"Phil is, was and always will be a complete weirdo. From 'To Know Him Is To Love Him' onwards, I mean, I used to hang around with Ronnie back then. She was really Phil's girl of course, he being that colossal Svengali-figure. But still, I mean, when Mick and I got to New York, first thing we'd do is get a cab down to Harlem - 127th Avenue, it was, and… uh… 'get it on', so to speak. But at the same time we'd be recording with Jack Nitzsche who we all know was Phil's arranger. And Phil would be hiding somewhere in the studio just glowering at me. He's just a very, very jealous guy." (1974)

Jack Nitzsche

"He's just this *obsessive*… beautiful… freak… an American Brian Jones if you like. These great spates of rampant irrationality. Always was a gas working with him, though. I still remember playing 'Let's Spend The Night Together' on the piano using one finger - things like that. Personally I've always felt he was never given enough credit for his work with Spector. I mean, when you consider how vital the arranger was to those productions. The need to understand spacings for instruments and the weight of the sound itself." (1974)

Aretha Franklin

"I took a few months sort of thinking about it, then Aretha Franklin asked me to do 'Jumping Jack Flash' with her. And I thought, I know the tune! This gig shouldn't be too difficult! I think I remember the chords to that one! And over that period Steve (Jordan, co-producer of 'Talk Is Cheap') and I had been becoming friends more and more - this was about six months after Stu had died and the Stones had decided to take a break. So I said, well I gotta do something. I wanna play. This hanging about is one thing that could really put me in the bin. Doin' nothing, you know?

"The thing with Aretha was great, I really enjoyed doing it. The amazing thing about Aretha is there is this voice, which is almost like a national monument in America, and when she sings, she's chain-smoking. Dionne Warwick's another one who just literally lights the new one with the old one. And they've both got these voices! Maybe I should smoke more!" (1988)

Seventies punks and Eighties idols

"Many of the English punk records sound like our early records, and that sound is very hard to achieve nowadays. But it seems to be the sound many of them are aiming for.

"You end up with someone like Glen Matlock... bringing Ian McLagan into the Rich Kids' line-up. So straight away there's a direct connection with The Small Faces. There's no way you're going to break those connections: sure you get concerted efforts like The Sex Pistols, but that... was as much Malcolm McLaren as Andrew Oldham was our early high-powered publicist." (1978)

"I like U2. I like Bono very much. We've done a thing here and there together. I like Stevie Ray Vaughan. I still really like guitar players, not that that's particularly new in pop music chronology. INXS I like. I've always liked AC/DC and the fact that they're not pompous. I like people that know what direction they want to go in as opposed to what people might like. I can't stand people trying to second-guess the public." (1988)

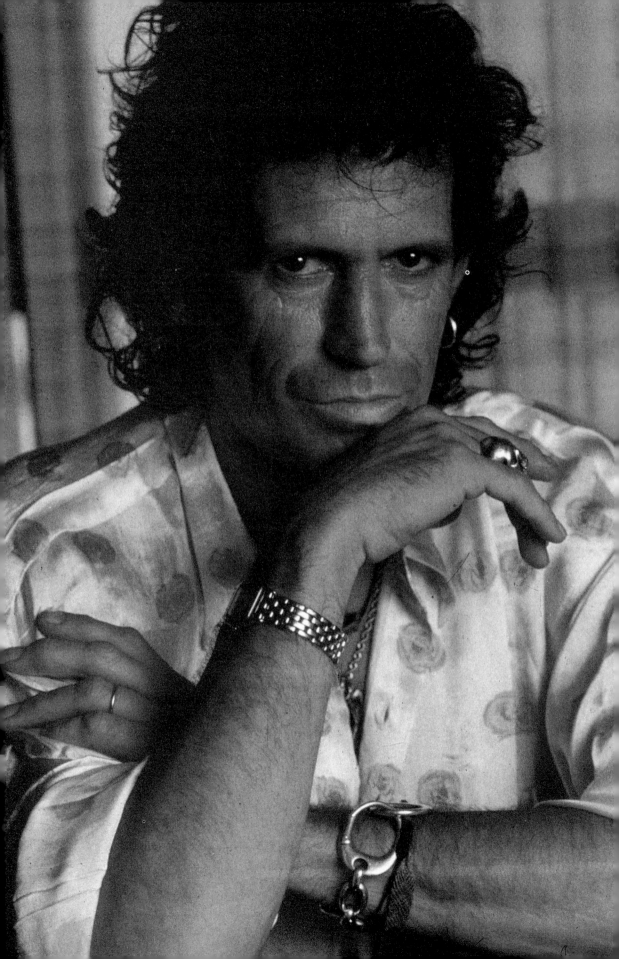

Blues & Rock'n'Roll

"R&B is a bit of a giggle. It's hard to say what R&B is. So many people say Chuck Berry is R&B, then he says he is rock'n'roll, so where do you go from there? Still I don't mind what you call it at the moment and for the next ten years. I'm happy." (1964)

"I reckon there are three reasons why American R&B stars don't click with British teenage fans. One, they're old; two, they're black; three, they're ugly." (1965)

"The Stones started as an idealistic blues band. We figured we'd do pretty terrible versions of real blues songs and, if people came to hear us, then they'd want to know where they came from and we could turn them onto our favourite music. Suddenly, we bypassed all that and we were rock'n'roll stars, and everyone started looking round at each other going, 'What happened, man?' But if you want to be a rock'n'roll guitar player, you've got to know yer blues." (1992)

"There's really only one song in the whole world, and probably Adam and Eve hummed it to each other, and everything else is a variation on it in one form or another, you know?" (1989)

"When someone in a tuxedo with greasy hair like Frank Sinatra comes along and records one of our songs then maybe we'll have a standard, too… the Irving Berlin type of music was founded on a basis of light opera and jazz. Our music is drawn from the influences of white and Negro folk music. We try to reflect forward-looking attitudes. You have to be progressive when you write for young people." (1974)

"They're out to make rock'n'roll illegal. Well, they've missed
another chance at it. Don't lock up the rock." (1978, after his
Canadian court trial)

"Music is a necessity. After food, air, water and warmth, music is
the next necessity of life. It's just the stuff to play it on that is a luxury.
And the PR and entertainment machinery that sucks off it, the leech,
is a distasteful element. But once you get into fashion in music it has
already diminished." (1988)

"At first you were aware that there was a powerful movement
growing, but it seemed to be only concerned with music. It only
appeared threatening on a minor scale, like riots inside theatres.
We didn't perceive the subversive power of rock'n'roll, that it carried
the seeds of something far more powerful – which came forth: rock
music became a political and social force. Maybe rock'n'roll had more
to do with breaking down Eastern Europe than anybody really wants
to give credit for." (1991)

"Does rock still have that revolutionary spirit? I'm sure it does.
You know, there were times when it was like the Stones were holding
a gun at the head of the world. Other times, it felt like the other way
round." (1992)

"I've always liked country music – you should never under-estimate
the importance of country in rock'n'roll." (1992)

 "The good thing about music is that it doesn't really matter – the
good thing about it is that it could fall apart any time.
    "It's a balancing act. But when you fall down you just get up again.
I guess I got over my embarrassment over falling down in public a long
time ago. Guilty your honour! That to me is what makes it interesting.
You set yourself up for a fall, you don't wanna fall, but you know you
can get up. Playing safe is not what it's about. This music is all about

beautiful fuckups and recoveries. That's why stuff like programming
is gonna strangle it to death. The best that programmed music will
ever be is 'not bad'. But we're not here talking now because music is
not bad. We're here because it's fucking great!…" (1992)

"Rock'n'roll is the rhythm of our generation. It's the epitome of the
kind of rhythm our generation grew up with, it's very natural to them.
As long as this generation carries on, rock'n'roll will live with it. But
now there's a new generation and it's searching for its own rhythm.
Each generation has its own rhythm.
    "Our parents had swing, we have rock and the kids of today are
taking our stuff and interpreting it for their time and their feeling of
life. We'll see where it takes us. Now, sadly, they've got typewriter
rhythms. People pushing buttons with fingers. But maybe that's the
feeling this generation has." (1991)

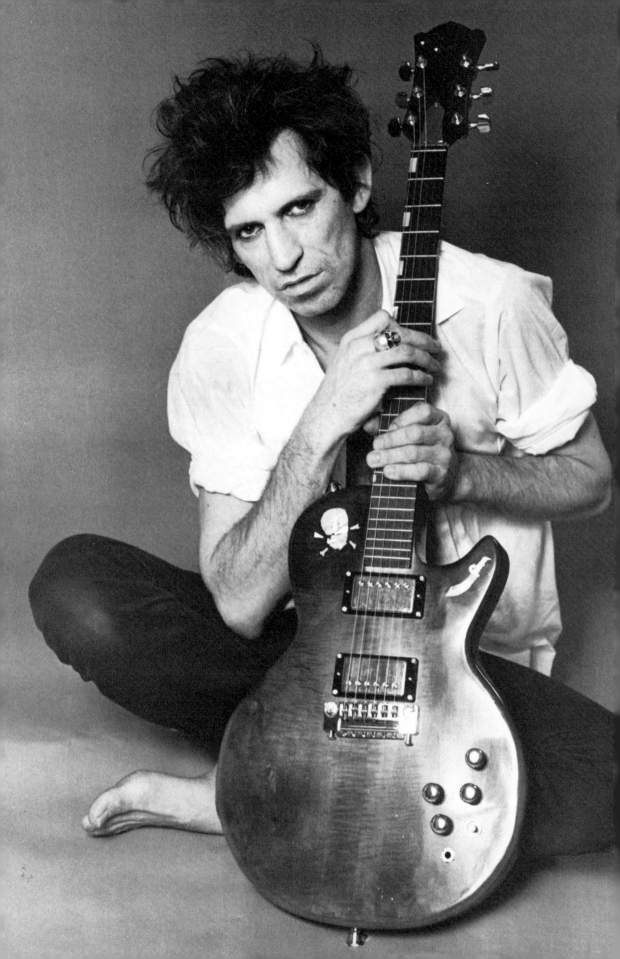

Guitars & Players

"I didn't say I was a rhythm guitarist, other people made my reputation for me." (1971)

"Gus Dupree, my grandfather on my mother's side, encouraged me by never pushing it on me. He used to play sax for a dance band in the Thirties. When I'd go to visit him, he had a piano and on top of it was this guitar. But it would only just sit there. He would never make any reference to it.

   "It was only a few years ago, in talking to one of my aunts, that I found out the guitar was only there when he knew I was going to come and visit: the minute I left it was back in its case. But I used to think it was a fixture, part of the house. But now you can see what a canny character he was." (1989)

"The Rolling Stones are basically a two guitar band. That's how we started off. And the whole secret, if there is any secret behind the sound of The Rolling Stones, is the way we work two guitars together."

"Brian worked incredibly hard with me in the very, very early days of putting the Stones together, and it was Brian and I who'd really got into the essence of this two guitar thing, of trying to get them to go into each other and you wouldn't care particularly who suddenly flew out and did a little line and that you could almost read each other's mind. But Brian also was the first victim of the star trip, and he went off the guitar very quickly, especially once Mick and I started writing songs together."

"I look at that guitar sometimes and think. There's only six strings and 12 frets, man. But the more you play it, the more things come out of it. Sometimes it seems so simple and you think, I could have done that 30 years ago! Things arrive in a strange order. If you can retain the mystery and turn-on of finding things out, then you can't put the goddamn thing down. It's too intriguing." (1989)

"There's no reason for my guitar being called Micawber apart from the fact that it's such an unlikely name. There's no-one around me called Micawber, so when I scream for Micawber everybody knows what I'm talking about." (1992)

"I'd gotten a bit bored, and I was getting a bit stale with playing everything on a concert tuning - you know, the regular six string thing - and I'd had the time to sit around and fool around and figure some of those old blues tunings and things like that, which I think is another reason why 'Beggars Banquet' suddenly had a slightly different sound to it, because that's what tunings and tonalities will

do for you. And my usual rap about the five string tuning – open
G tuning – is that you need five strings, you get three notes, you use
two fingers, and you get one arsehole to play it.

"But to me it rejuvenated my enthusiasm for playing guitar,
because you'd put your fingers where you thought they'd go and
you'd get accidents happening, and you wouldn't've done on regular
tuning, because you'd know it too well. You'd say, 'Well, that would
be wrong,' but then you just turn a few pegs and get a different tuning
and suddenly you get almost like a different instrument. It really gave
me a lot of renewed interest in playing the guitar." (1988 on 1968)

"My favourite Keef riff? I play it all the time! Every one's the same,
it's a variation on the same old thing!" (1992)

"I think I was born with the Keef riff, because to me it's 'Satisfaction' backwards, and I hear it in nearly every song that I do. It's in there somewhere. It's either reversed or dragged out in a different time or elongated, but I've wondered that myself. It's just there, you know. I can't give you a definite answer on that. Ask my ma or something." (1988)

"No guitar player can go wrong if they play acoustic guitar steadily, if they keep their hand in on the acoustic. If you keep the acoustic up, it'll help the electric guitar-playing. Otherwise you can get into that Fastest Guitar In The West syndrome, which is for rock'n'roll, absolutely a dead-end street. That's rock music, but it ain't rock'n'roll." (1989)

KEITH'S INFLUENCE

"I guess you got to start somewhere! I'm amazed there's so many of them that pick up on my thing. I'm glad I've turned that many guys on - but sometimes you think that what you were wearing is as important as what you were playing, it's such a double-edged sword. But that's all right too, when I started all I wanted to do was play like Chuck. I thought if I could do that I'd be the happiest man in the world." (1992)

"Bands have always been into copying us. I mean, what were bands like The Pretty Things and Them with Van Morrison doing back then?

   "Nah, it's not a piss-off and it's not particularly flattering either. I always wonder if they're just doing it for the bread or basic considerations like that." (1975)

"The Black Crowes used to send me tapes four or five years ago, They're a good little rock and roll band, what can I say? I don't think it's going to take anything to new heights, but then nobody expects to anyway. I can sympathise with them too, 'cause now they're The Black Crowes and that's what they gotta be. Once you become famous you kind of get arrested..." (1992)

The Sixties

"I've tried to put myself in the shoes of someone who wasn't there. You must have weird reverberations! And some of it's totally not true at all. I think in my time it would have been like talking about the roaring Twenties.

"Probably it wasn't anything like you'd expect. The Sixties were weird. especially if you were like The Beatles or ourselves, spending your life thinking wouldn't it be great if this happened, or this. And it did! Suddenly everything was going in line with what you'd fantasised, when you were laying around thinking 'wouldn't it be great to stir it up a bit!' But you didn't realise how big it was gonna get - you just wanted to shake them up a bit, not have any major revolutions or anything. What, you gonna have a revolution with a guitar, what you gonna do?" (1992)

"It was a painful year. It was a big year. 1967 was a year of change for everybody. 1967 was the explosion of the drug culture, if there is such a thing. That's when it came into the open from underground. Everybody started talking about it. And throughout this whole year, we were having to put up with this incredible hassle, this confrontation with policeman and judges. I feel very uncomfortable looking at a uniform anyway, and having to deal with these people for a whole year really did wear us down a bit. In fact, it put us on our back really for eighteen months or so.

"It wasn't until we got into 'Beggars Banquet' that the whole thing managed to slide into the past. Though at the time it was still bugging Brian like mad, and Mick. I suppose it was the fact that so many people, including the press, or sections of it, had been dying for so long to have a go at us. There are certain things which went on behind the scenes which are very unsavoury, and which once and for all destroyed my faith in the fairness and impartiality of the British judicial system. Only when you create a fuss and get it up to the highest level, then they start to reconsider." (1973)

"We carried a lot of things, being the focal point of a generation. But they've given us a lot of incredibly good times. Some fantastic experiences, and they are continuing to do so. Also, from being in that position, I've learned that if it turns you around, it turns round heavy. So you have to be prepared for that. That's probably the lesson I learned from 1967 and the whole thing." (1973)

"The Sixties were a really strange time, you know, things seemed to explode all at once." (1992)

Authority

"Subversive, of course we're subversive. But if they really believe you can start a revolution with a record they are wrong." (1969)

"What's on trial is the same thing that's always been on trial. Dear old them and us. I find this all a bit weary. I've done my stint in the fucking dock, why don't they pick on The Sex Pistols?"

"I bent down to change the waveband on the radio and the car swerved slightly. A police patrol vehicle then pulled out from a lay-by and stopped us. I was then questioned about having a 'concealed weapon', a penknife complete with tin-opener and a device for removing stones from horses' hooves." (1975)

"Like I said many years ago, I've never had a problem with drugs, only with cops." (1988)

"Once you were in the studio, you were virtually inviolable. You could lock the doors and just forget about a lot of the hassles that were going down. Whatever happened when you woke up the next morning, even if there were five officers waiting to wake you up... but that's another story.
"You could get away from the tensions and the confusion that was going on around that time, especially if you were used to travelling a little around the world and realised that at least the whole of the western world was pretty much in the same state, a lot of turmoil and confusion, with some people calling it revolution and other people calling it half-arsed anarchy. Really it was just chaos out there, so this was somewhere you had a little order going down and you could retain a bit of sanity for a while." (1988)

Relief on the forecourt, July 1965

"We never did anything consciously to shock people. All we ever did was answer the call of nature." (1979)

"I still maintain that it wasn't me. I just sat in the car and watched. The guys needed a pee and the guy said the garage was closed and they didn't have a toilet and Bill Wyman, who's the most famous pisser of all time - once he starts he can't stop - he's a little bloke and I don't know where he keeps the bladder but he just goes on and on, well he got nicked for it. The copper's saying, you're under arrest, son, and Bill's splashing it all over the copper's boots, he can't stop." (1988)

The Bust

"When the prosecuting counsel asked me about chicks in nothing but fur rugs, I said 'I'm not concerned with your petty morals, which are illegitimate.' They couldn't take that one…

"When it came down to it, they couldn't pin anything at all on us. All they could pin on me was allowing people to smoke on my premises. It wasn't my shit. All they could pin on Mick were these four amphetamine tablets he'd bought in Italy over the counter. It really backfired on them because they didn't get enough on us. They had more on the people who were with us that they weren't interested in."

Detained at Her Majesty's Pleasure, 1967

"Most of the prisoners were really great. 'What you doing in here? Bastards. They just wanted to get you.' They filled me in. 'They've been waiting for you in here for ages,' they said. So I said, 'I ain't going to be in here very long, baby, don't worry about that…'"

"So they took me to the governor's office and signed me out. And when it got up to the appeal court they just threw it out in ten minutes. The judge had just blown it. I mean, he said things to me that if I'd caught him by himself I'd have wrung his neck…"

Only in America…

"The first tour we did of the South, no-one was hung up on how genuine it was for us to be playing black music. Mainly, we offended white Southerners in those days because of our hair."

"We were arrested once for topless bathing. This was outside of Savannah, Georgia. Some people were driving by and swore that there was a load of chicks leaping in and out of the pool with just a pair of drawers on. So the cops came zooming up to bust these 'chicks', and of course the closer they got the more stupid they must have felt. Especially when they heard these South London accents saying, 'Aye, whattaya mean, mate?!'" (1989)

"The fact that a couple of American radio stations in Chicago banned the record ('Street Fighting Man') just goes to show how paranoid they are. Yet they want us to make live appearances. If you really want us to cause trouble we could do a few stage appearances. We are more subversive when we go on stage." (1968)

"I'm a very lucky man that I've never encountered any real problems with the American police. I think it's because they are now starting to understand. They realise what happened to Brian Jones, which was nothing more than sheer persecution. Hollywood is the end of the line for so many people. It's a killer and if you're weak you can be sure it'll get you. It's like when we were rehearsing in New York, we tried to find John Lennon and get him back into the scene. I mean, what the fuck is John Lennon doing farming cows in upstate New York? What's that all about?" (1978)

Corruption

"I don't get scared. I get mad. I haven't really been scared since I was at school, stood against a wall with the school bully in front of me saying, 'I'm gonna thrash you' and I'm saying, go ahead, what can I do about it? That's when I used to get scared.

"But when they (the police) were on to me, if I was scared it was on another level, not for what they were going to do to me - I knew the way they worked they couldn't make it stick, and would just make themselves look like idiots. I got scared for the rest of the country.

"I was brought up as a British schoolboy in the middle Fifties - and firmly believed Scotland Yard was incorruptible. Until I had to pay out ten grand and then get popped. And the scales fell from my eyes.

"They could do anything they wanted, and damn well tried. But the other thing that scared the shit out of me was how incompetent they actually were! The way they run the police force? The leader of a tribe of Boy Scouts has better intelligence than they have. It's so dumb! Their attempts at planting things, they'd find a little paper bag under the couch and go 'gotcha!'. It was like a Monty Python sketch, hello, hello, what do we have here? If I was running the police force and I wanted to knob somebody you'd be gone, no problem! But it was like being let loose with a bunch of Keystone Kops! And they're all on the take." (1992)

Sex & Drugs

"I was 19 when it started to take off, right, and just a very ordinary guy. Chucked out of night clubs, birds poke their tongues out at me, that kind of scene. And then suddenly, Adonis! And, you know, it's so ridiculous, so totally insane. It makes you very cynical. But it's a hell of a thing to deal with. It really is a bugger. Looking back now, happily married and all that, it seems incredibly funny, but it took me years to get it under control." (1974)

"I think chicks and guys have got more into each other, realised there's the same in each. Instead of them having to go through that completely hysterical, completely female trip to let it out that way (screaming). Probably now they just screw it out."

"They used to tell us 'There's not a dry seat in the cinema'. It was like that." (1971)

Getting high

"At first it was just a matter of something to make it to the next gig. It was like the old bomber pilot thing where they gave them Bennies to keep them going. Basically we would take them to get there and back. Then you get more and more fussy about what you're taking and you look for better, more… luxurious ones. You don't notice it. You don't give a damn about it. It's not necessarily a big deal.

"The drug thing has become a big deal now, and quite rightly so, because it's being pushed on kids. That, to me, is absolutely repulsive. But if you're a working musician then it's a different situation. No-one's pushing it on you. It's a high risk business for drugs." (1988)

"I'm tired of being number one in the naughty boys' drug poll. It's time they picked on someone else."

"People hate themselves anyway. If it wasn't smack they'd hate themselves for eating carrots. You can bet on it."

"People always try and generalise. You can sit 20 people around this desk, give them each five whiskies, and see how differently it affects these people. Some will be under the table, two will be completely sober, and another might be slightly tipsy. Everything affects people in different ways. My metabolism is just so fuckin' up."

"I don't know if I've been extremely lucky or if it's that subconscious careful, but I've never turned blue in somebody else's bathroom. I consider that the height of bad manners, I've had so

many people do it to me and it's not really on, as far as drug etiquette goes, to turn blue in someone else's john… " (1978)

"Dope or no dope, I've been doing the same gig. For the first seven years if I wasn't on the road I'd be sitting behind a desk like this, writing a few words, working out ideas, listening to some tracks, and doing what I'm doing now. I don't have to do anything different or lead my life differently just because I happened to take a certain amount of white powder. I never took smack to change anything."

"It's coming off the road and dealing with the withdrawal and expenditure of energy that does it. That absolute cut-off after two or three months on the road is difficult to adjust to. Coming back to a completely different rhythm was hard. And I found that smack made it very much easier for me to slow down, very smoothly and gradually.

"Otherwise I'd find I'd be glad to get home but I was still so hyper. I really wanted to enjoy relaxing at home. But I'd spend months wanting to enjoy, trying to enjoy but I couldn't. The one thing I can't handle really well is that sudden change of pace in living. I can handle it through slowing down or speeding up; that's easy. But I just haven't got any brakes…"

The guilt trip

"I never felt guilty about taking smack. I don't think anyone who takes smack feels guilty about taking smack. What they're really guilty about is something else. Some of them want to feel guilty. They *need* to feel guilty. And smack is the best thing to take if you want to feel guilty about anything. It's the perfect excuse to feel guilty.

"I've obviously felt guilty about things I've done in my life but not about or because of smack. If I felt guilty I wouldn't take it. The last thing I could bear is to feel guilty about smack."

"I don't like to regret heroin because I learned a lot from it. It was a large part of my life. It is something I went through and dealt with. I'd regret it if I hadn't dealt with it, or if I had OD'd. I would definitely regret it then. A lot of my friends, who should by rights be around, aren't, because of it. I don't think it made a damned bit of difference to anybody going to get into it being told 'don't'. In fact it sometimes reinforces the desire to take it. Having been on it I know. If there is anything I do regret, it's its accessibility to very young kids." (1982)

Cleaning up

"I cleaned up for the (American 1972) tour. But not for the
whole tour. I did take a bit. Playing isn't quite as much fun on smack.
But that's a difficult one 'cause it's not always true."

"I'm changing my image. I've arranged for a whole series of
dental appointments in Switzerland... I only ever get ill when I give
up drugs." (1974)

"I gave up drugs when the doctor told me I had six months to live.
If you are going to get wasted, then get wasted elegantly." (1974)

"Having treatment can be a very tough thing, but there are
certain medical advances that have been made which make it a lot
easier. There are ways of avoiding cold turkey with electro-therapy.
You know, all that rolling around the room in agony is for the movies.
You just go into hospital for two or three days. There are no needles
involved. They just use a small electric battery and circulate it between
your ears. The main problem is resisting the temptation to go back to
the stuff." (1977)

"If you want to get off it you will, and this time I really wanted it to
work. I've got to stay on the treatment if I want to stay off it for good,
if I want to kick it for good." (1978, during his Canadian court trial)

"I have grimly determined to change my life and abstain from any
drug use. I can truthfully say that the prospect of ever using drugs again
in the future is totally alien to my thinking. My experience has also had
an important effect not only on my happiness, but on my happiness at
home in which my son is brought up." (1979)

Above: Keith with Patti Hansen
Below: Keith with Tina Turner

"I cleaned up my act when I got busted in Canada in '77. I thought, I'm not getting off on it any more and also if I want to stay a free man, it's gonna have to stop." (1988)

"I never intended staying on it forever. I cleaned up because I wanted to. And that's the only way to do it."

Looking back

"Did I feel invulnerable? No, I didn't. I always gave a wry smile to find out I was number one on the death list. Because, knowing myself, I never considered I was actually pushing it anywhere near the danger limit, although later on I realised that I was probably a lot closer than I ever admitted. I always felt in control. But, hell, that's what that stuff (heroin) does to you. Suddenly finding yourself a rock'n'roll superstar, you need some place to hide, so I went in there as an experiment. But it was an experiment that went on far too long. But I don't regret it. It kept my feet on the ground. Nearly underground, in fact!" (1992)

"I would rather be a legend than a dead legend." (1988)

The Family Man

Keith the son

"Every time the poor guy (Dad) came in at night, he'd find me sitting at the top of the stairs with my guitar, playing and banging on the wall for percussion. He was great about it, really. He'd only mutter, 'Stop that bloody noise'."

"There comes a time in a guy's life when he has to fly the coop. At the time it was either him or me. Soon after that my mother and father broke up and Dad went his own way. I was working my arse off all over the world and we didn't keep in touch at all. Then slowly we started to make it up. A card here, a letter there. I'd send a note and a year later I'd get a reply, 'cos he never knew where to send anything because I'd be in one country one minute, another the next, or I'd be under arrest. I was thinking all the time, he don't want to know me, I've grown up to be the exact opposite of what he wanted me to be. Eventually we got back together again in '82 around the end of that tour. We'd been communicating a bit more over the month before and I got in touch and said, come down to my place, let's get together again if it's all right with you.

"So he agreed and I was still waiting for the guy I left 20 years ago. I expected him to get out of the car and - boom! - smash me in the teeth. That's how screwed up I was about it. At that time it was a very deep emotional thing, nothing you'd really detect on the surface. Then the car door opened and out stepped this little old guy and I thought, that's my dad. He came up and said, 'Allo son, haw ya doin'. And I'm breaking up already. Then I knew it would be all right. He lives up the road now and we have a game of dominoes some Fridays. I go up there and we have bangers and mash." (1988)

Keith the father

"I don't have to get schizoid about what I do and living a family life. We play music, the kids dance around. It's fun for them. And I enjoy, in my way, doing the odd family things, you know, like taking the kids out for a walk, going out to play with them. It's fun." (1991)

Opposite page: Three generations: Father Ben, Keith and son Marlon

"My kids are the straightest kids in the world. I've got a 19 year old son (Marlon) and he likes a drop of champagne now and then. He took care of me while I was doing heroin on the road. He used to be my roadie when he was five and six and seven. He's seen everything. To him it's not a big deal. It's just something Dad did. But we kept together and we love each other." (1988)

"When my youngest daughter was born, the doctor who delivered her came up in the dark, right after the birth, and held up five Stones albums for me to sign. It's a crazy world..." (1991)

Anita Pallenberg

"We had a great time in Rome when Anita was arranging *Barbarella*, but then we had to go to the south of France for the film festival and Brian again tried to engineer some scheme. Previously he had tried to engineer a reunion in Paris but Anita wouldn't have it. Anita was really upset. A couple of times she was in tears, which is very unusual for Anita. Maybe if Brian had handled it the right way, maybe he might have pulled it off. Whatever he did was wrong.

"During the première in Cannes I just stayed away and hung out in the hotel. Anita came back in tears 'cause Brian had tried to beat her up."

"Just because a chick leaves somebody to go with someone else is no reason to feel guilty. It happens all the time. It could have been someone 12,000 miles away but it happened to be the guy who stood on the other side of Mick onstage. And that's that."

"I refuse to get married because some bureaucrat says we must. Rather than do that I would leave Britain and live abroad. But if I want to continue to live in England, and if that's the only way Anita can stay, we will marry, but I don't know when." (1969)

"All you hear about me is when the warrants are out. What I resent is that they tried to drag my old lady into it, which I find particularly distasteful." (1972)

"Recording at my place was a necessity. The idea was to find another place to record, like a farmhouse in the hills. But they couldn't find anywhere so they eventually turned round and looked at me. I looked at Anita and said, 'Hey babe, we're gonna have to handle it'. We were clean when we went there. Anita had to organise dinner sometimes for something like 18 people. We redid the basement kitchen into the studio.

"And ever since then I keep hearing weird stories about how I'd disappear for hours but they knew very well what I was doing. I was putting Marlon to bed, which was very difficult with the whole fuckin' band thundering away down in the basement. Obviously it took me time to put Marlon to bed. The strain was mainly on Anita."

"I've been asked so often by the press and by both our families when we are going to get married that I thought we might as well. There are so many papers we have to produce, especially when we travel with the children, that it might just simplify things to have the same name on our passports." (1976)

"So many people are scared of our lifestyle. They're scared because they hold all their fuckin' problems in but Anita can't do that. She's gonna let it out. Anita and I will fight like mad. But at least we're honest with each other. If you've got to keep your problems hidden then you might as well not know the person in the first place. If you can't show yourself to the person you live with that's very sad."

Keith with Anita and Marlon

Home, There'll Always
Be An England

"Presley hit first. Actually, the music from *Blackboard Jungle*,
'Rock Around The Clock', hit first. Not the movie, just the music.
People saying, 'Ah, did ya hear that music, man.' Because in England,
we had never heard anything. It's still the same scene: BBC controls it.

  "Then, everybody stood up for that music. I didn't think of playing
it. I just wanted to go and listen to it. It took 'em a year or so before
anyone in England could make that music."

"We had to go through the same thing twice. In England we had
to slog round all the halls and ballrooms for a good year. We had our
first record but it was very much a snowballing process until it got
bigger and bigger. Suddenly we couldn't work in England any
more because the minute we'd get onstage the place was wrecked.
Absolute chaos. We'd play three songs and have to split."

"We're so excited at the prospect of doing Britain again after
so long. Wherever we might make our home now, Britain is where
our roots are." (1982)

"I can't forget that I am English. But it still pisses me off that they kicked us out of our own country. We didn't have the sort of money they were asking for, so we left. What really fascinated me was that they really thought three Herberts with guitars were a threat to the social structure of the country." (1988)

"I love England very much. I think Buckingham Palace would be my preferred residence. But they kicked me out! I've sold my place on Cheyne Walk 'cos it was falling apart. I sold it to some Arab who didn't know it was falling apart. They allow heavy traffic to go down the Embankment now. It's like a juggernaut route from Dover and they're shaking apart all those beautiful houses. They were meant to put a ring road or bypass there years ago but they were too stingy to do it. I used to try and redecorate that place but within three months the cracks would appear again. They're Queen Anne houses, man, they can't compete with heavy goods vehicles. So I flogged it to an Arab who'd probably never heard of Queen Anne.

"Since '66 I've had Redlands in West Wittering. That's real old.
They determined that the foundations were laid in something like
1130. They found a 14th Century wall when they were decorating and
got in touch with me in Hawaii and said, we've found this incredibly
old bit of wall, what do you want us to do with it? So I said, frame it.
And when I got there it was like one of the most beautiful paintings in
the world. It's got glass over it to protect it and it's beautifully framed.
It's just these old bricks with cow shit and straw holding them
together. A work of art! But Redlands is a beautiful joint. I'll always
keep that." (1988)

"I miss the smell of England, and because I know it so well it's the
only place I go to where I feel a bit of a tourist - it's all so familiar but
you notice every little change, every one-way street and the way
Nelson's Column is now white rather than black. And you kind of
resent feeling like that about your own place. But I'm sure that when
I do come home to roost it will only take me a few months and
I'll sink right back in." (1992)

Fame

Its drawbacks...

"I've had it with all that publicity. It's the kind of publicity I can do without 'cause everything that goes with it is very uncomfortable."

"Being famous is OK, but in the courtroom it only works against you."

"There's so much bullshit in the music business, all these pop stars. I almost prefer the 1961 style of interviews. Favourite colours or 'Helen bounced into the room'. Wasn't it amazing then? A star could do no wrong. Now you get sulking little creeps giving you shit."

"Everybody went through their star trip. I think Brian was the only one that it changed in a really deep way, and probably not for the better. He couldn't cope with it, really. It did change him almost immediately. Immediately, he started getting disillusioned. It was very difficult for him, not made any easier, probably, by the rest of us, because nobody had the time to look after somebody else. You've got your own trip you're going through.

"On top of that, you're working every night. If you're not working, you're recording. When that's going on for two or three years non-stop, it's all you can do just to keep yourself going. To look after another cat as well, it's impossible. That's one of the saddest things about stardom. And when it happens that fast, especially if you're in with a group of people, if one of them isn't quite strong enough to deal with that situation, there's very little you can do to help him." (1973)

"I always thought it was a miracle The Beatles and ourselves broke through the musical hierarchy to do what we did. Now I don't know if it could happen again, just cause there's so many people involved, and with money people it's all about safety. And good music is never gonna come out of that attitude." (1992)

... and its rewards

"After one thousand pounds comes ten thousand pounds – and then after that it means nothing. It's just a lot of money. You don't think about it… I suppose our most successful composition in terms of royalties must have been 'Satisfaction' which has now been recorded by over sixty different artistes all over the world, but we've no idea how much it has earned. It's still earning – I hope." (1974?)

"Rock'n'roll is a big business, you know. Musicians who find themselves suddenly the focal point of millions and millions of dollars neither have the time nor the inclination to be able to look after it all properly. You do need somebody to do it. Unfortunately, the record business, like a lot of other businesses, is run by a lot of very sharp people. There again, the thing I've learned, and it's a very simple answer, is that with anything involving bread, the only real way is to take anything that's offered to you and give it to an independent lawyer, and let them look it over.

"It's a very simple answer, but it's taken us a long time to learn it. I'd be the Maharajah of God Knows Where if I'd had all the money that we'd earned. It's a very sore point, because on top of the things that you've been through, to see good friends and people still being led by the same – how can I put it? – still being involved with what we know to be a very dodgy situation, and to see it still going on, when we'd hoped that, knowing what we've been through, people would be a little more wary." (1973)

Keith with Richard Gere and Robert Cray

"The whole area of rock'n'roll business and politics is a very, very tough game. If you can get into it, you find that you've no time for anything else. So the best thing to do is what we did, which was to ignore it as much as possible, and just hope for the best. That's really what it comes down to, you just hope for the best and learn what you can along the road to protect your own interests. That's all you can do. You can never possibly learn the whole thing and still be a musician. So rock'n'roll musicians always get the bad end of the deal." (1973)

"You can't whitewash the Stones. None of us minds the bread, but there's absolutely no way you could get Charlie Watts or, for that matter, any of us out there just for the bread alone. Our motives are musical. Everyone in the Stones still loves the music they're playing, and individually, still don't think they're good enough as musicians. But we're still trying to better ourselves. Now, whether we actually achieve it or not is always open to debate. But if we retain this genuine enthusiasm, then maybe we can go on and face the future with a brave face!" (1991)

"I figure I've made enough money to manoeuvre and do what I do without worrying about the business aspect. Though I wouldn't say I'm above it all - more like below it." (1992)

Growing Old

"Would I have seen it going on this long? No. That was one of
the things that worried me when it all started to happen, you know,
Stones-mania, and all that period. Up to that time, nobody had a life
expectancy of more than two or three years. Apart from Elvis. So I was
worried that it was all going to be over within a couple of years, when
I was only just starting to learn it and dig it. But things have changed
since then, and as far as I can see now, we can carry on doing what
we want to do and let it grow and mature and so on for quite a while.
So I'm quite hopeful that as long as I want to do it, I can do it. If we
want to stop, we can, but I don't see any diminished enthusiasm from
anybody, so I feel we'll go on for a while." (1973)

"We know a lot of the old black boys have kept going forever.
A lot of the old black boys, the blues players, as far as we're concerned
they're virtually playing the same thing. They kept going until the day
they dropped... There's no denying there's a high fatality rate in
rock'n'roll. Up until the mid Sixties the most obvious method of
rock'n'roll death was chartered planes. Since then drugs have taken
their toll, but all the people that I've known that have died from so-
called drug overdoses have all been people that have had some fairly
serious physical weakness somewhere.
    "I feel very hopeful about the future. I find it all very enjoyable...
with a few peak surprises thrown in. Even being busted... it's no
pleasure, but it certainly isn't boring. And I think boring is the worst
thing of all." (1978)

"Nobody ever turned around to Muddy Waters, BB King or
John Lee Hooker and said 'Now you have got to stop; you're not
allowed to play any longer'. I played with Muddy just six months
before he died and I'd never heard him play better - still powerful
because he knew how best to conserve his energies in a different way.
This was a man at the tail end of his life, yet still able to perform with
such creativity." (1991)

"I'm not a kid any more, and I've thought to myself how long can
I keep doing this? That's the great thing about it - the not-knowing.
But within the narrow confines of rock'n'roll, it's for me to find out
how to use my experience and produce something that hopefully is still
worth listening to. Like I said, somebody has got to find out how far
you can take this thing, and I guess it might just as well be me!" (1991)

"When I was 20 or 25, the idea of reaching 30 seemed horrific.
Suddenly, you're there and you put it up to 40! Then suddenly you're
there. I'm more philosophical now..." (1988)

What Others Say About Him

Family

"(Grandfather) Gus had this guitar standing in the corner and he was always afraid Keith would break it when he touched it. Keith went up and strummed the strings. He loved that b-b-broom sound of the guitar. Keith positively admired Gus." (Doris Richards, Mum)

"Keith always sang to the radio or a record. And he knew all the words. At Christmas if I didn't sing a grace note Keith would tell me to do it properly. He'd know it was wrong. It's something that's just built in him." (Doris Richards)

"I worried about Keith because of that awful place in Edith Grove. They'd stay in bed all day because they had no money for the heater, food or anything." (Doris Richards)

The Stones

"I distinctly remember this conversation I had with Keith. We lived in the same block and I asked Keith what he wanted to do when he grew up. He said he wanted to be like Roy Rogers and play guitar. I wasn't particularly impressed with the Roy Rogers bit but the part about guitar did interest me. It was obvious even then that Keith really was interested in guitar." (Mick Jagger)

"Basically I came from the same sort of background as Brian and Mick: middle class and fairly well educated despite my Cockney accent. I'd never really been exposed to anyone like Keith before. He was a complete layabout with an art school education." (Ian Stewart)

"I'd say Keith was shyish. He always was shy. But you shouldn't exaggerate it too much because in a lot of ways he was also outgoing. He has his moments of being shy. Maybe it's just being Keith." (Mick Jagger)

"Keith doesn't like anyone to think he's shy. He opposes that by being over confident. Actually, the more I get to know Keith the shyer he seems to be." (Bill Wyman)

"Keith is the sort of guy you should leave alone. He's the classic naughty boy. He's the sort of guy I knew at school who hated the head boy. And I love Keith because of that." (Charlie Watts)

"Despite the fact that class was very important it never separated me and Keith. We're very similar because we come from the same place. Keith and I were always close. We still are.

"I've never known anyone as long as I've known Keith. Therefore I've got nothing to compare it to." (Mick Jagger)

"Keith was the best dressed of them all. In England nobody wore Levi's except Keith's period of art students. The way Keith dresses is amazing. Often I'll put on one of his belts or something made of tapestry and it looks fuckin' ridiculous on me. Keith has beautiful style. He has a way of putting clothes together that I'd never dream of. Often Keith will wear one of Anita's blouses or waistcoats and it will look amazing." (Charlie Watts)

"Keith liked The Beatles because he was quite interested in their chord sequences. He also liked their harmonies, which were always a slight problem to The Rolling Stones. Keith always tried to get the harmonies off the ground but they always seemed messy. What we

never really got together were Keith and Brian singing back-up vocals. It didn't work because Keith was a better singer and had to keep going 'ooh, ooh, ooh.' Brian liked all those 'oohs', which Keith had to put up with. Keith was always capable of much stronger vocals than 'ooh, ooh, ooh.'" (Mick Jagger)

"Keith is the musical leader. He is in charge of recording sessions more or less in an oblique way. He doesn't march into the studio and say, 'Right, it's gonna be this, that and the other and you'll play it like this and that.' He just kicks off into something, most people follow him. He usually decides how a song is going to shape up."
(Ian Stewart)

"Keith is confident because he doesn't try to be anything he's not. Keith liked the fact that smack made him feel good and laid back. And it made him feel more confident. It made him able to stick his fingers up at a bum note no matter who was watching or what they thought 'cause underneath you knew it was good."
(Ron Wood)

"In terms of leadership Keith is obstinate. If things don't suit Keith, he simply won't go along with it. And that's the end of the subject. There was no liaison. No, 'Should we do that?' It was simply, 'No.' And when asked 'Why not?' Keith would reply 'Cause I don't want to.'" (Bill Wyman)

"I don't know how much I need or depend on Keith as I've never had to do without him. I'm sure both of us could do very well apart. But we work as a team." (Mick Jagger)

"Keith represents an image of what the public thinks the Stones are like. Gypsy, pirate, drinking, smoking, finally heavy drug taking, swearing. People see Keith and they see the Stones."
(Bill Wyman)

"Keith was a bit like Charlie. Keith would find one girl and pretty much stick with her. He's been the same way ever since. Maybe a few here and there but nothing like Brian and Bill who went potty over birds." (Ian Stewart)

"Once Keith was going to marry a girl just to get into America. Just pick a random name. I figured Anita would have either been up for the prank or whacked him one. But Keith was game to try. Incredible." (Charlie Watts)

"Keith will always flog himself on stage. Keith never coasted on stage. Some nights he'll move and other nights he'll just stand and play. Some nights he might be a bit out of it and drop the odd clanger but he never coasts." (Ian Stewart)

"Maybe all the publicity does encourage Keith 'cause he is so much a Rolling Stone and leads that lifestyle and does so to justify himself. But it has a bad effect on people because when they think of Keith they think of drugs, nothing else. There's a lot of other junkies and it's a purely private personal problem anyway. No amount of busts or publicity will change a thing. There will always be a part of Keith that reacts to people telling him what to do. If he quits smack he's got to want to."
(Mick Taylor)

"Keith is different when he's in public, when the group are performing, when we're under public scrutiny. When you're in a restaurant on tour there's an excitement about the upcoming show. People are aware that you're in town and you've got to keep up the appearance. When you're not on tour the atmosphere in a restaurant can be very relaxing. Half the time they don't even think the person they're looking at is Keith Richards. It's quite easy for him to blink."
(Ron Wood)

"Though Keith is more sensitive than I, we didn't have any major rows. We're not an old married couple who can't live together and can't live apart; we're two men who've been friends for 30 years. Occasionally you want to strangle even the closest of friends."
(Mick Jagger)

"Even though they try to keep up, Keith puts them all by the wayside. Keith has great bravado. Although he likes drugs, what is to his benefit is that he takes them seriously. He doesn't fuck about with them. That's why Keith can function. He won't mix them up. Keith has a thing about chemicals. He doesn't like them. Keith's got it down."
(Charlie Watts)

"I don't think Keith wants the world to acknowledge him as the leader of the band. He wants to be the leader with Mick as the figure-head. Mick can have all the glory he wants. Keith just wants the band to sound the way he thinks it should sound.
   "Keith is the leader of the band until such time that Mick will walk into a studio with a song that's written and finished. If it's Mick's song and he's got it stuck in his head how it's gonna be it'll be done usually." (Ian Stewart)

"Keith and I are very good friends. Not only friends but we work together as well. We may have arguments but our friendship always continues." (Mick Jagger)

"Keith's whole street image is self-destructive but that's not Keith really. His public image tends to be a bit punk but he really isn't harmful at all." (Ronnie Wood)

Other musicians

"At first you got the impression that Keith was just trailing around with Mick. The first 15 minutes he was trailing around but it didn't take long to realise Keith wasn't trailing around at all. He just happened to be quieter." (Alexis Korner)

"All these bands that talk about their wild lifestyles – Keith Richards invented it. He's done everything. There's nothing that can impress that guy. And he's still doing it.

"Keith Richards is the epitome of rock'n'roll. He drinks like a fish. After the shows he drinks with his mates and jams to blues records. He just loves the blues. Before he goes on stage you hear him warming up with all these blues licks. He lives for his guitar and his Jack Daniel's and his Rebel Yell.

"You see the Stones crew some mornings and they're hungover and you say, 'What's wrong wi' ya?' And they say, 'We were out with Keef last night – never again.' And then you see Keith roll in and he's fine." (Paul Elliott *Support group Gun, 1990*)

"Keith always used to wear a purple shirt, jeans, pointed shoes, and a jean jacket. That's all he'd ever wear. Day in and day out he'd wear that purple shirt. I've got a distinct memory of sitting on the bus watching Keith walking up the hill to school on a really cold day. He'd be strolling along, never wore an overcoat. Never saw him in anything else." (Dick Taylor *original Stones bassist*)

"Keith wanted to do it his way. He was perfectly right. Besides, there wasn't much opportunity for Keith to play. Blues Incorporated basically were not a guitar band, which The Rolling Stones became." (Alexis Korner)

"Keith wasn't shy as much as he was quiet. I could make him laugh but most of the time nothing was funny to him. He was very much himself in his own room and his own world. He really is a bit of a softie." (Ronnie Spector)

"Keith is the only one who is not naturally middle class. Keith is a man of belief. This is meant merely by way of contrast. Keith is a man of belief and Mick is a man of fear. Mick works on fear, that driving thing, 'What if I fuck up?' It's a lot easier to be like Keith than it is to be like Mick. A lot easier." (Alexis Korner)

"Without Keith's rhythm guitar there wouldn't be a Rolling Stones. Keith is the Stones. He's got all those riffs and that sound which is The Rolling Stones. What Keith does is play guitar without trying to be flash. It's all taste. And playing for real. Keith plays real rhythm guitar without any bullshit. Keith doesn't make a lot of faces. Ever notice Neil Young? He makes faces like he's doing something spectacular. I hate guitarists who make faces without doing anything." (Jack Nitzsche)

"Keith has his own way of working. He works on his own emotional rhythm pattern. If Keith thinks it's necessary to spend three hours working on a riff, he'll do it while everyone else picks their nose. I've never seen him stop and explain something."
(Glyn Johns *co-producer, 'Get Yer Ya Yas Out'*)

"Keith takes risks which makes the whole thing worthwhile. Why bother unless you fuck up? Human beings fuck up. Mick's big risk isn't his performance. His big risk is his political situation. He always rides the risk of the Stones no longer being able to function; Mick has taken the big upfront political risk. As far as legal risks, Keith is the renegade." (Alexis Korner)

"Keith has these endearing little habits. I love the way he cuts his hair. It's continual. Every day when we were on the plane he'd look at all the little toys in his bag, pull out some scissors and just pick up chunks of his hair and cut it. He was always cutting his hair. I think he told me once he'd never been to a barber."
(Gary Stromberg *Stones' American PR man*)

"I didn't know who he was. Keith didn't get kicked offstage, he was just playing too loud. And I asked him to play softer. I thought the cat had something but I couldn't even recognise him. After a song I said to play softer, play down. So I start the song and it's loud. On the next song I just said, 'Off.' Then my secretary is offstage screaming at me 'That's Keith Richards.' I said, 'Oh no, go get him.' But ya see the latter didn't make the papers. I think they split before the show was over. I'd like to play with the Stones though if the circumstances were right." (Chuck Berry)

"Keith lives with danger but it's not self-torturing. There's a curiosity about it. You can only learn so much from your experience, depending on how much you want to learn. And Keith wants to learn a lot." (Alexis Korner)

"He's still in love with his music, and literally the lines disappear from his face when he picks up that guitar." (Bono)